Time Gentlemen, Please!

The Story of Winchester's
Pubs, Breweries and Hotels
past and present

by
Phil Yates

Phil Yates

This book is published by The City of Winchester Trust Ltd
Winchester Heritage Centre
32 Upper Brook Street Winchester SO23 8DG
Registered Charity No. 251798

Supported by Hampshire County Council

ISBN 978-0-9555271-0-4

Cover Illustrations:
Front: Clockwise: *The India Arms, Railway Inn, Old Market Inn* and *The Foresters' Arms*
Back: Pub signs two of which no longer exist, *The Chimneys* and *Prince of Wales*.

Printed by Sarsen Press, 22 Hyde Street, Winchester SO23 7DR

This book is published to celebrate
the 50th anniversary
of the formation of
The Winchester Preservation Trust
now known as
The City of Winchester Trust
1957 – 2007

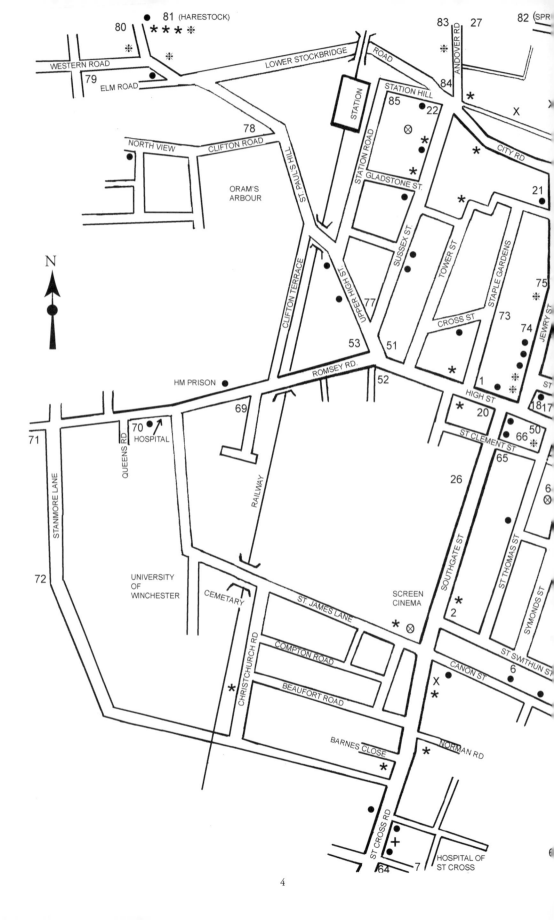

CONTENTS

LIST OF ILLUSTRATIONS

Please refer to the map on pages 4 and 125 for the location of venues numbered in this list.

INTRODUCTION

The summer evening walks organized by Nick McPherson on behalf of The City of Winchester Trust have grown in popularity over the years with locations ranging from the Hospital and Chapel of St. Cross and Winchester College to Winchester's Churches, past and present and The Village in the City (Hyde).

On the final tour of the 2004 season, which took place at The Grange, Northington, suggestions for new venues to be incorporated in the 2005 programme were requested. I proposed Winchester's pubs, breweries and hotels, past and present; consequently I found myself researching this fascinating subject in order to conduct a tour during that summer – which turned out to be in two parts!

So, in June and August 2005, armed with notes and photographs, I proceeded to take a group of 35 members on both occasions around the sites of Winchester's pubs, breweries and hotels, finishing at *The Westgate Inn* on 9 June and at *The Hyde Tavern*, a traditional venue for the Trust's conclusions of tours and farewells, on 25 August. During a conversation that evening, over a drink – or two – with Patricia Edwards, Chairman of the Trust, and Nick McPherson, the 50th anniversary of its formation arose. As part of the commemorative celebrations an idea came into their heads; this book is the result of that idea!

The information for my tours, the articles which appeared in the *Hampshire Chronicle* at the start of 2005 and for the book, have been obtained by dipping into the archives and unearthing some valuable details, especially from *Warren's* and *Kelly's* Winchester Street Directories spanning several years, and Ordnance Survey Maps, produced by the staff of the Hampshire Collection (formerly the Local Studies Library). In addition I have inspected many old documents and plans produced by the staff of Hampshire Record Office. I am indebted to both staff members who were extremely helpful; so were some publicans – over a drink – with customers joining in to help out!

I have restricted the area of public houses, breweries and hotels, past and present, which existed in 1900, and since that year, to within the city's boundaries. However, some watering-holes which operated long before the commencement of the 20th century, have crept into my findings.

I am sure older citizens will recall a number of public houses which disappeared many years ago while newcomers to Winchester have the advantage and opportunity of visiting the remaining venues.

Perhaps I should explain the reasons for choosing the four pubs shown on the front cover. Firstly the colour schemes have changed since those photographs were taken in 1996 and secondly, *The India Arms* has since become *Alfie's* and *The Foresters' Arms* is now *The North Walls*.

Although every effort has been made to record correct details in the book, I apologise for any discrepancies or omissions, which may occur. This is due, mainly, to the fact that neither the Hampshire Collection, the Hampshire Record Office or I have been able to ascertain, in our researches, the information required.

All references to pubs, breweries and hotels (i.e. names and owners), are indicated by italic printing.

The more observant reader will, no doubt, spot that names of some venues referred to in the List of Illustrations and in the chapters that follow are not preceded by the definite article "the", (i.e. *Mash Tun, Railway Inn* et al). The reason? This is how the wording appears on the façade of the premises or on signboards. Therefore, to be authentic in every way, and to comply with the photographs, I have, where appropriate, deliberately not put this word in italics.

Having said that, it has given me great pleasure, as a member of the Trust, to write this book as part of the celebrations to commemorate its 50th anniversary. I hope you enjoy reading the contents – cheers!

Phil Yates
March, 2007.

The second edition of this book has been revised and, so far as possible, brought up to date.
Phil Yates
November 2007.

ALCOHOLIC QUOTATIONS

Here are some quotes about "drink" by famous authors: -

It's my opinion, sir, that this meeting is drunk, sir!
Charles Dickens – *The Pickwick Papers* (1837) Chapter 33 – Mr.Stiggins

Doth it not show vilely in me to desire small beer?
William Shakespeare – *Henry IV, Part 2* (1597)

Alcohol.... enables Parliament to do things at eleven at night that no sane person would do at eleven in the morning.
George Bernard Shaw – *Major Barbara* (1907)

An Alcoholic: A man you don't like who drinks as much as you do.
Dylan Thomas – Constantine Fitzgibbon – *Life of Dylan Thomas* (1965)

There are two things that will be believed of any man whatsoever, and one of them is that he has taken to drink.
Booth Tarkington – *Penrod* (1914)

It was my Uncle George who discovered that alcohol was a food well in advance of medical thought.
P.G. Wodehouse – *The Inimitable Jeeves* (1923)

What have you been doing in my absinthe?
Dick Vosburgh – *A Saint She Ain't* (1999)

And, finally, this quote could apply to any one of us on a bad day:

But I'm not so think as you drunk I am.
J.C. Squire – *Ballade of Soporific Absorption* (1931)

DID YOU KNOW?

Visitors to Britain's shores frequently comment that there is nothing quite like the English pub to be found anywhere else in the world. Alas, the rural pub is under siege. One 1999 estimate suggested that such establishments were closing at the rate of six a week. In some rural areas, where the village shop no longer exists, pubs are now having to take on other tasks to stay afloat, adding, for example, a post office and other shop facilities.

The introduction of hops into brewing brought a new drink on to the market – "beer". Ale was still the premier booze since it was unadulterated with preservative hop flowers added to beer. Recognising a good thing when they saw it, the Dutch and Flemish immigrants, who had settled in England, took advantage of the situation to develop hop gardens in counties like Kent and Sussex, and these became well established by the middle of the 16th century.

"Tied" houses came into being through the endeavours of William Simonds, one of the early brewing monopolists (see chapter 3 regarding *Simonds' Brewery* of Reading). Until William arrived on the scene the wholesale beer and ale market did not really exist because of laws laid down in the reign of James I. These generally prohibited wholesale supply of beer except to fully licensed establishments. Sensing that times were changing William sought out potential positions for hostelries in the south of England. When the law changed in the early part of the 1800s he was able to move quickly and set up fifty alehouses to take his wholesale product.

Finally, in 1900 the cost of a pint of beer served in a public bar was 2d. in old money – today's average price for a similar pint of beer – £2.90p.

CHAPTER 1
The way they lived

The social way of life in our city over a century ago was very different from today. By the late 19th century Winchester's town centre witnessed the expansion of infilling through the erection of small houses and the destruction or divisions of larger residences.

In the poorer areas of the city dwellings were overcrowded and in need of repair. Although regulations for new buildings with drainage and provision for bathrooms and toilets came into force, older houses erected prior to the introduction of such regulations were denied these facilities which resulted in large families residing in small terraced houses. Parts of The Brooks, for instance, were so bad with dilapidated buildings and poor drainage that in 1903 many of the old dwellings were demolished. In Middle Brook Street, for example, houses were pulled down and thirteen new ones constructed that year in the cul-de-sac known as Prince's Buildings for tenants of Winchester Cottage Improvement Society, the equivalent today being Winchester Housing Group. There was a notice on the wall of one of the houses which read "Football and Cricket are forbidden" – today the notice just reads "No Ball Games".

The working class lived in terraced houses in areas like The Brooks, St. John's Street, Canon Street, Water Lane, Wales Street, Wharf Hill and part of Colebrook Street.

1. *The Talbot Hotel* on the corner of High Street and Staple Gardens. This photo was taken c.1895 after the original *Star Inn* was rebuilt. The name changed to *The Talbot Hotel* in 1929. Your Move, estate agents, now occupy the premises.
    Photo: Winchester Museums, Winchester City Council

Several public houses or beer-houses were situated in each terraced street – eighteen in The Brooks alone – five in Canon Street – four in Wharf Hill – and so on, as you will discover in chapter 8.

With the lack of indoor entertainment such as cinemas, radio and television the inhabitants of these areas relied on other leisure pursuits. The children played out in the roads with hoops which they rolled down the street where vehicles were a rare occurrence. Outdoor recreational facilities included riverside walks, open spaces and parks at St. Giles's Hill and Abbey Gardens where there was a small aviary. The statue of Queen Victoria (1887) by Sir Alfred Gilbert, sculptor of Eros in Piccadilly, once adorned the Gardens before being removed to the interior of the Great Hall of the former Winchester Castle in 1910. The recreation ground and public park at North Walls was still at planning stage in 1903.

Another outlet for occupiers of these small terraced houses was the consumption of cheap alcoholic drink; consequently the increase in public houses rose so rapidly from ninety-seven in 1880 to one hundred and thirty-two in 1902, within the city boundaries alone – twenty-one of them being in High Street!

Demolition of older inns took place and they were replaced by typical "designed" pubs of the period. Two examples come to mind; *The Star* on the corner of High Street and Staple Gardens was pulled down and rebuilt in 1885, the name changing to *The Talbot Hotel* in 1929, and *The Green Man* on the corner of Southgate Street and St. Swithun Street was replaced in 1881 by a smart city tavern as seen today. More details about these pubs can be found in chapter 8.

2. *The Green Man*, on the corner of Southgate Street and St. Swithun Street. Rebuilt in 1881 for Richard Moss from designs by Thomas Stopher Junr. *Photo: Author*

In addition to the astounding number of public houses for a city the size of Winchester whose population in 1900 was 21,500, the town also boasted five breweries in that year, although over a period from 1852 to 1925 there were ten in operation, the last one being *Hyde (Winchester) Brewery* which ceased brewing beer that year. Adjacent to most breweries were "taps" or "taprooms" – at least six existed in Winchester!

If that wasn't enough, several individual beer-houses were scattered around the city. These consisted of houses where beer was often sold in the kitchen of the occupiers' home. They would sell beer by retail to be consumed either on or off their property. Drinking spaces in people's homes were separated, seating being available in the "taproom", but standing space only offered in the "bar-room". The more genteel might look for an establishment with a parlour!

Some beer-house keepers found themselves in serious trouble with the law. The occupier of 47/48 Lower Brook Street, for example, was summoned in March 1898 for "keeping open licensed premises during prohibited hours"; the verdict? Case dismissed. But the occupier of 33 Sussex Street wasn't so lucky. Summoned for the same offence in May of that year, he was committed and "fined 10/- with costs of 11/- or 7 days"!

In addition to "taps" and beer-houses a number of malt-houses were spread over a wide area of the city including Busket Lane, Swan Lane, Hyde Street, St. Cross Road and St. James' Lane.

Ten hotels, five of which were temperance – in other words abstinence from alcoholic drink – served Winchester. Like the breweries, some of them ran their own "taps" in adjacent premises or separate bars; I refer to all the "taps" that I can trace in chapters 3 and 8.

But the interest of the public in the watering-holes of the city started to decline in the early 1930s when another form of leisure became popular – more about that in the next chapter!

CHAPTER 2
The way we live

The first indication of indoor entertainment arose in the late 1920s and early 1930s when the wireless became an essential part of the household furniture for most families in the country but that did not stop the "regulars" from popping round to their "local" for the usual nightly "tipple". In fact radio sets were installed in public houses so that they could listen to their favourite programme while enjoying a pint and a fag or a pipeful of tobacco!

Although films had been shown commercially at The Palace, a cine-variety theatre in the banqueting-hall of the 13th-century St. John's House on The Broadway since 1910, it wasn't until sound was introduced in 1927 that the tide began to turn, and for 6d. or 1/-, families could enjoy three hours of pure entertainment "at the pictures". Every cinema offered the hope of escapism for its audience and they were also centres for the local community.

The fast-growing film industry in Britain and America led to the building of new large cinemas throughout the country and the city benefited from the erection of the Odeon on North Walls which opened in 1933, (retirement homes called Richard Moss House occupy the site today), and the Ritz, the last cinema in the country to be built after the commencement of the Second World War; this opened in April 1940. The building, situated in Middle Brook Street, has now been transformed into Winchester Family Church. There had been four other cinemas operating during the "boom" years – the Picture House (now Superdrug), the Royal, converted back to a theatre in 1978, the Regent, the newly refurbished Winchester Discovery Centre, and the New, on which part of Winchester School of Art is built. So, citizens were well catered for in this alternative form of entertainment.

By the 1960s, however, the onslaught of television gripped the nation from which not only cinemas but also pubs suffered with a drastic fall in attendances. It was inevitable that many hostelries closed only to be converted into private residences or offices. A worse fate befell many of them, as well as cinemas – demolition. But for those pubs which survived, a change of tactic from an ordinary drinking venue was required.

Prosperous inns added function rooms and private rooms where business could be discussed away from the bustling city centre,and so it was that hostelries created a social role for themselves thus resulting in the introduction of "bar food", attracting customers to stay and enjoy one another's company. The experiment proved so successful that most pub owners had extensions built or converted part of the interior of their premises into restaurants and outhouses became skittle alleys. Any exterior spaces were turned into beer-gardens.

Regular features now included quiz nights, with pubs competing against each other, and live music performed by bands from various parts of the county. The boozers are now well equipped with darts, pool tables, large TV screens scattered around the bars mainly for sporting events, fruit machines, video juke-boxes and even a quiz machine!

Pubs, like cinemas, may be fewer in number, but they are thriving especially with the new 24-hour drinking law, which came into force on 23 November 2005. A total ban on smoking in these venues commenced from 6 a.m. on 1 July 2007. Smokers having a cigarette in public face on the spot fines of £50 and premises that allow smoking will be fined up to £2,500! Lighting up will be outlawed in all enclosed public places in England, including 200,000 pubs and restaurants.

There is one consolation, however, for the "regulars"; bans on poker games in pubs since the 1960s was lifted in 2007 and although new regulations will insist that pub poker tables host only two-stakes games, there will be no policing of pub gambling to prevent stakes being raised to high levels.

The public houses within the city's boundaries now amount to forty-five with six hotels, and another one proposed, but regrettably no breweries exist in Winchester. Cinema attendances are also on the increase with the opening of multiplexes in various parts of the country; they also include bars!

Now I will take you on a journey around Winchester to trace pubs and hotels, past and present, and the sites of the breweries that I deal with in the next chapter.

3. The Picture House, High Street, now Superdrug. Photograph taken c.1935.

Photo: Winchester Museums, Winchester City Council

CHAPTER 3
The city breweries – all past

Part of a large brewery once occupied the site of Avalon House in Chesil Street. *Chesil* or *Cheesehill Brewery* fronted this street and extended at the rear to face the forecourt of the former city station of the Didcot, Newbury & Southampton Railway on which the Chesil Street car-park now stands. The brewery was operated by *Pointer & Son* from 1852 to 1898 when it was acquired by Benjamin Bishop Colson who continued the business, trading under the name of *B.B. Colson & Co. Ltd.*, until 1920. The company also owned nine public houses which are referred to in chapter 8. The section of the brewery, now occupied by Avalon House, was converted into a laundry called Snow White Electric Laundry in 1927, which had previously used the premises, now known as The Bridal Room, since 1914. The laundry closed in 1973 and the buildings were demolished in the late 1970s. Avalon House was built in 1988 and opened in 1989.

The word Chesil is a corruption of the old English word "ceosel" meaning "gravel" and this part of Winchester was built on a natural gravel bed, similar to the Chesil Beach at Portland in Dorset. In the 18th century the name was changed to Cheesehill because cheese is said to have been rolled down the hill from the Fair held on St. Giles's Hill but there is no record that this ever took place! The name reverted to Chesil in about 1916. This district of the city is known as The Soke, which was under the jurisdiction of the Bishop of Winchester until 1835.

4.   The *Chesil Brewery*, Chesil Street. This photo shows the offices of the brewery c.1880.
Photo: Winchester Museums, Winchester City Council

Not far away in Eastgate Street on the corner of Friarsgate (originally Boundary Street) stood the *Lion Brewery* on the site now occupied by Greyfriars Flats. This was operated by Peter Punton until 1880 after which time Francis Hill Punton ran the business. In 1895 *Wootten & Co.* acquired the premises, first trading under the name of *Lion Brewery Ltd.* and subsequently under the name of *Lion Brewery (Winchester) Ltd.* After brewing ceased in 1931 the Winchester & District Co-operative Society acquired the building in 1933 for their bakery and continued this use until the early 1960s when demolition took place. Greyfriars Flats were built in 1964, although it was the Black Friars who, after making their appearance in England c.1221, were given a foothold in this area of the city called Coytbury where they acquired property c. 1264. The name applied to the area of ground of the Black Friars' precinct and may have been a personal name. A fulling-mill existed in the 13th century and a new one was constructed in 1402. Why are the flats called Greyfriars and not Blackfriars? A possible answer is that the Greyfriars coaches operated from a garage on the opposite side of Eastgate Street for many years. Incidentally, the offices of NHS Practitioner & Patient Services Agency on the corner of Friarsgate and Tanner Street is called (sic) Coitbury House!

5. The *Lion Brewery*, Eastgate Street. Photo taken c.1960 when the buildings were used by the Winchester & District Co-operative Society for their bakery.

Photo: Winchester Museums, Winchester City Council

The original brewery sustained two major fires during its existence, the first being on 16 November 1879 after which much reconstruction was done; large additions were made to the buildings and plant in 1896. The second fire on 14 August 1908 caused considerable damage to the south side (High Street end) of the brewery. This was discovered by an employee of the Gas Company (a lamplighter) shortly after 3.30 a.m. on his rounds extinguishing the street lamps. A notice appeared in the *Hampshire Chronicle* at the time stating that there would be "no interference with the business in any way".

The *Lawn Tap* stood on the site now occupied by Lawn House residential flats for the elderly.

The other brewery connected with *Wootten & Co.* stood on the corner of Southgate Street and St. James' Lane which was known as Barnes Lane until the 19th century. The brewery, called *St. James' Brewery*, sometimes referred to as *Southgate Brewery*, made an impressive building. The area consisted of 47,500 square feet with extensive frontages and included a ten-quarter malt-house. The brewery had been in the possession of the Barnes family for many years. The premises were fitted with a fourteen-quarter plant and machinery worked by a steam engine. The brewery was put up for sale in April 1860 by Richard Moss, at that time residing in London, (see next chapter). *Dear & Co.* then ran the business until 1887 when it was acquired by *Wootten & Co.* who operated the plant until 1900 when the brewery finally closed. The malt-house was in St. James' Lane on the site now occupied by dwellings known as Southgate Villas whilst the brewery stood on the site of Wessex Tandoori Indian Cuisine Takeaway, The Golden Lion Chinese Restaurant and part of the garage formerly known as Will Short Ltd. but now called Southgate Peugeot.

Before embarking on the next brewery I should explain that *Wootten & Co.* was formed and registered as a limited liability company in 1895 to control the *Lion* and *St. James'* breweries. The company's name changed to *Lion Brewery Ltd.* in 1900 following the closure of *St. James' Brewery* and to *Lion Brewery (Winchester) Ltd.* in 1906. The company was acquired by *Strong & Co. of Romsey Ltd.* in 1931 who ceased to brew on the plant at Eastgate Street.

The *Queen's Brewery*, according to the 1873 Ordnance Survey map, stood on the site now forming part of The Brooks Shopping Centre in Upper Brook Street and was a prominent feature of the city centre. A two-storey building, the brewery existed from c.1859 to the early 20th century. As part of the major redevelopment of the area in the late 1950s and early 1960s the premises fell victim to the scheme and was demolished to make way for the city centre car-park prior to the erection of the Shopping Centre which opened in February 1991. The *Queen's Brewery Tap* formed part of the brewery.

Looking towards Symonds Street on the right-hand side of Little Minster Street, just beyond King's Head Yard, was *Sadler's Brewery*. The premises backed on to St. Thomas Street where St. Thomas House now stands, which was built c.1890 as The Winchester Institute. The brewery is known to have existed between 1867 and 1880. A large flint building, it was used after 1880 for many years as The Winchester Temperance Billiards Hall. The premises were taken over in 1952 by Bendicks for its chocolate manufacturing factory until the company moved to its new purpose-built production unit at Moorside Road, Winnall in 1967. Bendicks, famous for its Bittermints, was founded in 1930 in a shop in Kensington. The building in Little Minster Street, which had five-bayed windows on the upper floor, was demolished and replaced by new apartments and garages. The architect obviously took into consideration the five-bayed windows, which were reinstated, complete with a roof garden, as seen today.

Continuing along this street we come to Symonds Street, named after Peter Symonds, the founder of Christ's Hospital (1607); the 6th Form College, which bears his name, was founded in 1897as a school for boys. Facing the street are two terraced houses, Nos. 23 and 24 St. Swithun Street, which were, in the 1800s, *St. Swithun Brewery.* I ascertained very little information from documents produced by Hampshire Record Office but these properties are clearly marked on the 1880 Ordnance Survey map as *St. Swithun Brewery.* It is quite possible that a family occupying both houses used part of the premises for living accommodation, and the remainder for brewing purposes! As a child, I visited my aunt who resided at No. 24 – she never mentioned anything to me about living in part of a former brewery – still, I was only 8 years old at the time!

6. *St. Swithun Brewery*, St. Swithun Street. A small brewery existed at Nos. 23 and 24 St. Swithun Street in the 1800s.   *Photo: Hampshire Chronicle*

Carrying on down St. Swithun Street and through the 14th-century Kingsgate, with the church of St. Swithun-upon-Kingsgate, we come into College Street and the approach to Winchester College, founded by William of Wykeham on 20 October 1382, its first stone being laid in 1387, the year in which Geoffrey Chaucer began his *Canterbury Tales.* The flintstoned building extending almost the entire length of the college frontage to the porter's lodge was the college brewery. All the beer was brewed here for the consumption of the Warden, Fellowes, Scholars and Quiristers. A considerable amount was consumed, according to the figures of the *Liber Actorum* of 1709, which reads thus: "There was brewed yearly in Winchester College about 820 Hogshead of small beer the value whereof doth amount yearly to about £100". After allotting 70 hogsheads to the Warden and a generous allowance to scholars and servants of various degrees "348 hogsheads were consumed in a manner not to be accounted for". The first reference to hops occurs in 1542; these were foreign hops, far too expensive for the college funds, and so in 1564 hops were planted in the "Sick House Mead" at the rear of the buildings with the object of supplying a certain quantity which could be augmented as required by purchase. The mead, however, was laid down to grass in 1619 but brewing continued to 1904.

The definition of hogshead in the dictionary is "a unit of capacity, used especially for alcoholic beverages. It has several values".

Returning from College Street under Kingsgate Arch and through The Close gate, we approach Pilgrims' Hall, built in the 17th-century as part of No.3 The Close. This building was used as a "Common Brewhouse" for the Dean and Chapter of Winchester Cathedral before being adapted to serve as the Dean's stables and coach-house. The Hall was restored to its original state in 1959 whilst No.3 The Close, a former canonry house, became Pilgrims' School in 1931, whose 75th anniversary celebrations took place on 30 September 2006.

Leaving The Close under the archway to the passage leading to Colebrook Street we pass an impressive house (No.1 The Close), built between 1698 and 1728, but at the rear stood a dwelling originally known as No.2 The Close, a canonry residence purpose-built c.1541. Among its occupants was Canon Thomas Ken, well-known hymn writer, later Bishop of Bath and Wells, best known for his refusal to give Nell Gwyn, an actress and mistress to Charles II, permission to stay at the house on an occasion when the King visited Winchester. The grounds for refusal were "that a woman of ill-repute ought not to be endured in the house of a clergyman". She was, instead, accommodated in a suite of rooms at the south end of the Priors' Hall. Charles Layfield, a successor to Thomas Ken, occupied the house from 1689 to 1710 and "bore the share" of converting part of it ("No. 2A") into two brewhouses for the residents of Nos. 1 and 2 respectively. This long building remained in use, first as a pair of brewhouses, and later as a washing-house, until the mid-19th century. The last occupant of No.2 was Canon Edward James who died in 1854. By that time the house was in a dilapidated state and beyond repair so it was demolished in the Spring of 1856, the site of which together with its garden were added to No.2 The Close (Deanery Cottage) which now houses the offices of The Friends of Winchester Cathedral.

Snook's Sussex Brewery stood a short distance up a narrow lane that led to the railway station from Sussex Street. The site is now engulfed by Hampshire Record Office. The brewery consisted of a small brick two-storey building, which existed between 1859 and 1867. No other information was available on my research.

I found another problem when researching the *Water Lane Brewery*. According to documents at Hampshire Record Office the brewery was situated in Water Lane on the side of the River Itchen now known as Riverside Walk, not far from the bridge spanning the river connecting Water Lane to Eastgate Street close by the *Mash Tun* public house referred to in section I of chapter 8. The brewery was in existence from 1808 to 1859 with a frontage to Water Lane and a depth stretching to the bank of the river. It became a private residence in 1859 and the whole area was demolished in 1958/9 for the creation of Riverside Walk. The *Water Lane Tap* was incorporated within the brewery building. But, according to the 1880 Ordnance Survey map, the brewery was situated on the other side of Water Lane adjoining the passageway, which leads from the lane to St. John's Street at the rear of the oldest parish church in Winchester, St. John the Baptist, dating from the 12th century. The Tap formed part of the brewery, which closed c.1885, but it would appear that the Tap continued trading until c.1924.

From Water Lane we come into Wales Street and at the far end, just before arriving at the public house known as *First In Last Out,* referred to in section I of chapter 8, is a car-park belonging to The Winchester Housing Trust. On this site stood *Winnall Brewery* which was conveyed by William Etheridge to Benjamin Colson in June 1887, before he acquired *Chesil Brewery.* William Etheridge had carried on the business of a brewer for "the last 50 years upwards". The premises consisted of a four-quarter brewery built on two floors with a beer-house (tap) adjoining. It closed in 1898 and became a mission hall the following year until 1908 when the building was transformed into a laundry, similar again to *Chesil Brewery.* Subsequently, the premises were demolished and a new laundry built c.1919 known as Winnall Laundry which continued until the early 1960s when demolition took place and the whole area was redeveloped, except for *First In Last Out.* On the other side of the public house is a cul-de-sac called Colson Road named after the famous brewer.

The Hospital of St. Cross was founded by Henry de Blois between 1132 and 1136. Besides housing "thirteen men, feeble and so reduced in strength that they can scarcely, or not at all, support themselves..." a further one hundred poor men were fed each day in a building a short distance away from the almshouses. The present structure, dating from the 14th century, no longer being required for its original purpose, was converted into a brewhouse in 1782. I would like to think that the brethren brewed their own beer there! The Hundred Men's Hall has now been tastefully transformed into tea-rooms and is situated on the left-hand side of the outer quadrangle, near the outer gate. Henry de Blois, the grandson of William the Conqueror, was Bishop of

7. *The Brewhouse*, St. Cross. Situated in the outer quadrangle of the Hospital of St. Cross, formerly The Hundred Mens' Hall, now tea-rooms. *Photo: Author*

Winchester 1129-73. In 1446 Cardinal Beaufort, half-brother of Henry IV and Bishop of Winchester 1404-47, refounded the Hospital.

Under the arch of the Beaufort Tower is the porter's lodge where at the gate, visitors who request it are given the Wayfarer's Dole following the unique ancient tradition founded by a Cluniac monk whose Order always gave bread and wine to travellers at a time when St. Cross stood on an important east-west route for merchants and pilgrims. Today the Dole consists of a small beaker of beer and a morsel of bread.

A brewhouse, dating from the 1600s, also existed at No. 75 St. Cross Road, a few doors away from the *Gardener's Arms* (see section VII of chapter 8).

Two large breweries in Hyde Street were on opposite sides of the street and practically faced one another. According to the 1880 Ordnance Survey map there was a malthouse off Swan Lane and on its corner with Hyde Street stood Denmark House, the site now occupied by Homerise House residential apartments. Further down Hyde Street on the left-hand side was a public house by the name of *Brewers Arms* (not to be confused with the pub of the same name in Chesil Street) – (see section I of chapter 8). Beyond this inn stood a small brewery called *Neville's Brewery,* with another malthouse at the rear. Hugh Wyeth, a brewer and maltster, purchased the premises in 1869 and promptly demolished it including a small red brick house where his father had a baker's business. He erected a new large four-storey brewery building on the site which he named *Hyde Abbey Brewery.* This was designed by father and son architects Thomas Stopher and Thomas Stopher Junr. Roman and medieval remains were found on the site prior to the commencement of building works, the contract price being £2341. A new malt-house was built at a later date. Hugh sold the premises in 1897 to

8. *Hyde Abbey Brewery*, Hyde Street. Hugh Wyeth, the original owner, sold the brewery to *Welsh & Co. Ltd.* in 1897. This photo was taken in 1903.

Photo: Winchester Museums, Winchester City Council

Welsh & Co. Ltd., having previously moved in 1891 from his private residence at No. 79 Hyde Street to the New Forest. Always keen on theatre, he set up a company of amateur actors to perform Shakespeare's works and returned to Winchester on several occasions with his company. The name *"Welsh"* appeared in bold white lettering on the high brick wall of the brewery to which alterations and additions were made in 1900. *Welsh & Co. Ltd.* was taken over by *Coopers* of Southampton in 1929 which later became part of the *Watneys* group of breweries. The *Brewery Tap* adjoined *Hyde Abbey Brewery*. The buildings were converted into commercial premises in the early 1930s. Richardson & Starling Ltd., the woodworm specialists, occupied them from 1940 to 1983 when demolition took place. The present building, known as *Wyeth House,* was opened in July 1985 and consists of flats for the Kingfisher Housing Association. The name *"Wyeth"* is imprinted in the brickwork over the main door of the premises.

In February 1943 a lone German bomber dropped a string of bombs, which fell close to the old buildings; this resulted in casualties, some fatal.

Finally, the last brewery to operate in Winchester, known as *Hyde Brewery,* comprised a large area on the east side of the street. There had been a brewery on this site since the early 18th century. Nicholas Pye operated it until 1812 when the premises were acquired by John Waight who rebuilt the brewery in 1821. By 1850 James Simonds, brewer of Reading, operated it renaming the premises *Simonds' Brewery.* Richard Moss, a brewery valuer from London, purchased the complex in 1863 naming it *Hyde Brewery.* He formed a limited liability company called *Winchester Brewery Co. Ltd.*, which was registered in November 1893. Richard Moss instigated alterations and additions to the premises in 1904. After serving the community in many ways for over 30 years he died in March 1905; more information about this remarkable gentleman is contained in the next chapter. The company, along with 108 licensed premises, was taken over by *Marston Thompson & Evershed Ltd.* of Burton upon Trent in 1923.

Brewing ceased in 1925 although bottling continued until 1964. For seventy years the brewery was used as a distribution centre only, the alcoholic beverages being supplied by *Marston's*. The logo on all pub signs was eventually changed from *Winchester Brewery Co. Ltd.* to *Marston's* – for short!

Transportation of supplies from Burton upon Trent to Winchester was by road or rail. As many as ten wagons loaded with beer arrived daily at one time at the Bar End goods yard of Winchester Chesil on the Didcot, Newbury & Southampton branch line which closed in 1960. Thereafter lorries drove through the night with their cargo arriving at the North Walls entrance of *Hyde Brewery* early the following morning, leaving by the Hyde Street exit the same evening for the return journey to Burton upon Trent.

The depot closed in 1995 and the premises, including the site of Hyde Abbey Tennis & Bowling Club adjacent to the brewery, were sold to Banner Homes for residential development, the whole area being demolished in 1996.

All traces of the original buildings have vanished except for the *Counting House,* now converted into private dwellings with the frosted windows on the Hyde Street side still containing those words. The *Counting House,* entered through the beer-garden of the adjoining inn, *The White Swan,* was a place where tenants of the brewery's pubs came to pay their rents, which usually consisted of coinage only – hence the name *Counting House.* The other part of the building still surviving contained offices, the board room and the strong room where the deeds of all the company's properties were kept until transferred to *Marston's* at Burton upon Trent. The massive "omnibus" deed containing all the freehold and leasehold pubs and other properties of the company journeyed up and down the country on many occasions – usually tucked between crates of beer on the lorries! It was my misfortune to have the task of collecting it, along with other deeds, because the firm of solicitors where I was employed as a Legal Executive acted for *Winchester Brewery Co. Ltd.* and *Marston's* for many years.

The site, on which the apartments and houses are built, called appropriately Marston Gate, opened in 1999 although the original name given to the area was Winchester Gate. All the company's pubs were acquired by the *Greene King Brewery* of Bury St. Edmunds in 1999 – another change of logo on pub signs to *Greene King*!

9.   *Winchester (Hyde) Brewery,* Hyde Street. A general view of the brewery in 1972. Demolished in 1996, the site now contains apartments and houses known as Marston Gate.

Photo: Winchester Museums, Winchester City Council

The house adjoining *The White Swan,* No. 86 Hyde Street, was the General Manager's residence, one of whom was Donald Willitts. His son David grew up there and as a youngster he found a stone in one of the cellars bearing the date "1704", the year when the brewery was founded. The house is now privately owned. *The White Swan,* formerly part of the brewery site, now operates under the banner of *Greene King*; more information about this pub is contained in section XVI of chapter 8.

The two entrances to the original brewery now form part of the Marston Gate development, the main one being via Hyde Street. One last snippet of information before leaving the chapter on the city's breweries is that James Cagney, the Hollywood actor famous for portraying gangster roles in films, paid a visit to the brewery in 1942 – why was he in Winchester? You can find the answer in section I of chapter 8.

10. One of the frosted windows of the *Counting House, Hyde Brewery*, Hyde Street, still visible today. The property has now been converted into private dwellings.

Photo: Hampshire Chronicle

CHAPTER 4
Pillars of the Community

The inspiration of two astute businessmen was responsible for the expansion of the brewing industry in the city during the second half of the 19th century, which included the refurbishment or replacement of public houses and, as disclosed in the previous chapter, the reconstruction and extensions to *Hyde Abbey Brewery* and *Hyde Brewery*. The names of these gentlemen were Richard Moss and Thomas Stopher Junr. This chapter is dedicated to them.

Richard Moss

Although not a Wintonian by birth, Richard Moss became a prominent figure in Winchester through his many involvements serving the community and by the time of his death in 1905 he was described by the *Hampshire Chronicle*, reporting on his passing, as "the greatest philanthropist and benefactor Winchester has had among its citizens during the present generation".

Richard Moss was born in London on 30 May 1823 and on leaving school he became an "apprentice to John Wright Snow, citizen and scrivener of London" consequently marrying his daughter Mary in 1858.

For many years Richard was head of an important firm of brewery valuers in London and his first association with Winchester came in 1860 when dealing with the sale of *St. James' Brewery* (see previous chapter). Three years later in 1863 he purchased *Simonds' Brewery*, renaming it *Hyde Brewery*.

His first residence in the city was on Station Hill before moving c.1880 to Northgate House in Jewry Street. The property is situated at the rear of Canister House and has now been converted into flats. In 1884, however, Richard and Mary with the family (two sons and a daughter) moved to Weston Grove overlooking Southampton Water. From there they moved to live, for a short while, at Stoke Poges in Buckinghamshire before finally settling at "Fernhill", Blackwater, near Farnborough.

Richard soon took an active part in the affairs of his "adopted city" serving on the City Council representing the Ward of St. John from 1872 to 1878, and in 1880, as a Conservative candidate, he was returned as one of the two Members of Parliament for Winchester, the city having two members in those days. When the next general election came in 1885 the representation for Winchester had been reduced to one seat but due to health reasons Richard did not stand. However, a by-election took place in 1888 on the death of Col. Tottenham, the existing MP, and he was elected for the second time to represent the city for the Conservatives with the greatest number of votes ever recorded by a Parliamentary candidate. After Richard retired from the political scene in 1892 his proudest moment came the same year when he was elected the second

Honorary Freeman of the city of Winchester, the first being the Earl of Northbrook. Richard was already a Freeman of the city of London, elected in 1845. Why wasn't he ever Mayor of Winchester? He could have been in 1874, but at that time "party feeling was very strong in the Winchester City Council and the Liberals were in a considerable majority".

As mentioned in the previous chapter, Richard formed a limited liability company in November 1893 called *Winchester Brewery Co. Ltd.* and he remained chairman of that company, which controlled *Hyde Brewery* until his death.

During the ownership of the brewery he undertook, with architect Thomas Stopher Junr. the rebuilding of three public houses in the city, *The Green Man, The Dolphin Inn* and *The Crown Hotel* as well as the construction of the De Lunn Buildings adjoining the hotel. Please refer to chapter 8 for more information concerning the last-mentioned pubs and buildings.

Amongst other things, Richard provided a soup-kitchen for the poor and transport to take poorer citizens to the County Hospital to visit their sick relatives. He also gave to the city the railings around the Abbey Gardens.

For nearly 30 years Richard was secretary of the County Brewers' Society and took a prominent part in the amendment of the Licensing Laws of 1869 and 1872. The following year he became Warden of the London Scriveners Company where he had started his career as a young man some 30 years earlier.

By a Trust Deed dated 22 January 1903, Richard Moss transferred to the Mayor, Aldermen, and Citizens of the city of Winchester, and I quote, "17 fully paid-up 6 per cent preference shares of £100 in the *Winchester Brewery Company* to pay the income of shares yearly to the Mayor for the time being to assist him in dispensing the hospitality of his office and partly to defray the expenses of a banquet or other entertainment to be given on 30 May in each year or as near thereto as conveniently may be, being the date of the birth of Richard Moss, to the Mayor Aldermen and Citizens and visitors as the Mayor may invite". This document was sealed in the presence of J.A. Fort (Mayor), B.D. Canceller (ex-Mayor) and Walter Bailey (Town Clerk). I inspected a copy of the deed, which is lodged at Hampshire Record Office.

The memory of Richard Moss, Freeman and benefactor of Winchester, is honoured to this day in Abbey House, the Mayor's official residence, on or near to 30 May in every year, when the Mayor entertains members of the City Council and other guests. The annual ceremony of toasting Richard Moss is held in accordance with the bequest of him to perpetuate the city's recognition of its generous benefactor. On 30 May 2006, the 183rd anniversary of his birth, I attended the ceremony in Abbey House. Standing by his oil painting, given to the city by his family, the 807th Mayor of Winchester, Councillor Sue Nelmes, proposed the toast "to the memory of Richard Moss". Displayed close by on a table was the silver epergne presented to him on 12 June 1874 by the County Brewers' Society in recognition of his services as secretary of that organization for nearly 30 years. Used as a centrepiece for a dinner table, an epergne is normally crafted in silver with a large central basket or dish, flanked by either candle brackets or smaller dishes (or baskets) for sweets, savouries and fruit. The Moss Epergne, presented to the city by Mrs. A.E. Moss in March 1943, is also used for the Retiring Mayor's Dinner, which is usually held in May of every year.

This adopted son of Winchester died on 2 March 1905 at his residence "Fernhill" within three months of his 82nd birthday from "failure of the action of the heart". At the time of his death he was High Steward-elect of Winchester.

The funeral, held at Holy Trinity Church, was attended by representatives from all walks of life with whom Richard had been associated. Crowds gathered in the Broadway as the cortège processed, with the sound of muffled bells from the cathedral, to the place of interment at the old Morn Hill Cemetery, "immediately outside the entrance to the mortuary chapel (on the south side) – a beautiful spot overlooking part of the city and the picturesque valley to the south".

In the account of the great man's death the *Hampshire Chronicle* of 4 March 1905 stated, "One who knew him most intimately described him as being then a fine, handsome man, with keen blue eyes that seemed to read the character of his fellows well-nigh at a glance, but beneath the man of business was the kindly genial personality that endeared him to everyone with whom he came in contact through his life".

The retirement homes on North Walls opened in 1990 are appropriately called Richard Moss House and overlook the famous brewery he acquired all those years ago.

Thomas Stopher Junr.

Born in the small Suffolk town of Saxmundham on 3 June 1837, the year Queen Victoria ascended to the throne, Thomas Stopher Junr. was the son of Thomas Stopher, a master-builder who came to Winchester in 1839 to supervise a large contract for Winchester College and later became Clerk of Works on the construction of the new Winchester Prison on Romsey Road (1846-49). Subsequently, he was appointed County Surveyor for Hampshire and resided at 21 St. Swithun Street.

His son was educated at Trafalgar House School, now Hampshire County Council Social Services, in Trafalgar Street. On leaving school he entered his father's office as an architectural pupil and after a while started practising as an architect which he continued to do for over 50 years in the city at 57 High Street which he shared with the *Hampshire Chronicle.*

Besides his "partnership" with Richard Moss, Thomas was responsible for the construction, alterations and additions to many properties in and around Winchester. He succeeded his father as Surveyor to the Governing Bodies of Winchester College and to the Trustees of St. John's Hospital.

Like Richard Moss, Thomas took an active part in the affairs of the city becoming a city councillor in 1872, a position he held for 44 years until his death in 1926. He was Mayor of Winchester three times (1876, 1883 and 1893), made an Alderman in 1883 and became an Honorary Freeman of the city in 1910.

He was a gubernator (governor) of Christ's Hospital and as such had much to do with

11. Richard Moss (1823-1905). MP. for Winchester 1880-1885 and 1888-1892. Founder of *Winchester Brewery Co.Ltd.* Honorary Freeman of the City of Winchester and Benefactor.   *Photo: Winchester Museums, Winchester City Council*

12. The Moss Epergne on display at the Richard Moss ceremony held on 30 May 2006 at Abbey House.   *Photo: Author*

13. The Mayor of Winchester (Councillor Sue Nelmes) and Deputy Mayor (Councillor Chris Pines) standing by the portrait of Richard Moss in Abbey House at the ceremony held on 30 May 2006.
      Photo: Author

14. Elizabeth Hickish, granddaughter of Thomas Stopher Junr., standing by the oil painting of her grandfather in Abbey House during her visit to Winchester in October 2005.   *Photo: Hampshire Chronicle*

the founding of Peter Symonds School in 1897. But perhaps his greatest achievement both as an architect and as a city councillor was his involvement in the improvement of the sanitation of the city from a cesspool system to proper drainage carried out at the cost of £32,000.

A distinguished member of the Masonic Order, Thomas held several offices in the Lodge of Economy No. 76. He was also a local historian and, among the many contributions he made in the way of scrapbooks and other papers, were detailed notes of several properties in High Street which have assisted me in research for this book.

A generous person, Thomas was instrumental in setting up one of the county's first free lending libraries and reading rooms in the city and his life-long collection of books, etchings, paintings and items of antiquity were always available for scholars to see.

Thomas married three times, the first two wives predeceasing him. His first marriage to Mary Frances Hendy in 1861 produced two daughters and a son; the second one to Louisa Carey Brown was childless and finally in 1900 he married Edith Stobbs who survived him with one daughter.

He resided for many years at "Chilcombe Chine" on St. Giles's Hill, which was one of a number of houses in that area which were designed by him. He died there on 2 May 1926 within a month of his 89th birthday and was working until a week before his death, which was caused by congestion following influenza.

The funeral service in Winchester Cathedral was attended by members of the City Council, Masonic Brethren and representatives from the many charities and organizations with which he had been associated. It was followed by burial at "the new" Magdalen Hill Cemetery which opened in 1914.

Before the commencement of the monthly City Council meeting following Thomas's death, the Mayor (Councillor Hayward) said: "He was a man with high purpose and one we always looked up to for guidance in many things. His broad kindly philosophy has helped me through many a hard day and often cheered me up".

I conclude this part of the chapter on a nostalgic note. In October 2005 Elizabeth Hickish, the granddaughter of Thomas, visited Winchester from her home in Cornwall to find out more about her grandfather. Elizabeth's mother, Betty, was the daughter from his third marriage to Edith. During her visit Elizabeth saw the oil painting of her grandfather in his mayoral robes which hangs in Abbey House and remarked: "It has been wonderful to meet people who are so knowledgeable about my grandfather and to learn about the influence he had on this city for over 50 years".

He was, indeed, a great man, and left his mark on the city along with his friend and the other "great" – Richard Moss.

CHAPTER 5
The county breweries – past and present

In addition to the breweries of Winchester, several that were located in various parts of Hampshire operated some of the city's public houses. Regrettably the majority of them, like the city's breweries, have also disappeared from the scene but, thankfully, over recent years new ones have taken their place and supply alcoholic beverages to public houses and other venues in and around the district of Winchester.

It is impossible to name every brewery, past and present, but this chapter is aimed to highlight some of the redundant and existing ones that were or are scattered around our county which had or have associations with licensed houses referred to in chapter 8.

Past breweries

I commence with *Strong & Co. of Romsey Ltd.* whose publicity was unmistakable when entering Hampshire travelling by road or rail. Large signboards, mainly in fields, clearly stated "You are in the Strong country." The brewery, located at Horsefair, Romsey, had been established since the late 1700s by Richard Trodd and Thomas Hall but it wasn't until 1858 that Thomas Strong leased the brewery and 28 licensed houses from the Hall family, then purchasing the business in 1883. Strong's were registered as a limited liability company in 1894. *Whitbread & Co. Ltd.* of London acquired the company, along with 950 tied houses, in 1969. Brewing ceased in June 1981 but the premises

15. The brewery of *Strong & Co. of Romsey Ltd.* in the 1890s.
Photo: Lower Test Valley Archaeological Study Group

continued to be used by them as a distribution depot until October 1989 when it finally closed. All the buildings were demolished except for two malt-houses dating from the 1890s for which, along with the tower, has been redeveloped for housing to create a "New Quarter" for Romsey.

The prominent feature when entering the picturesque village of Twyford through the meadows by the River Itchen is the steeple of the church but the village also possessed, at one time, a brewery. Situated on the main road by the corner of Park Lane the building consisted of a brewhouse on three floors and a malt-house on two floors. The Young family are known to have brewed there from 1859 to 1911 when the premises and its seven tied houses were acquired by *Eldridge Pope & Co. Ltd.* of Dorchester.

John May & Co. was registered as a limited liability company in 1894 to acquire the business of the same name that was operating *The Brewery* at Brook Street, Basingstoke, which had been established in 1750. The company was taken over, along with 90 to 100 licensed houses, by *H & G Simonds Ltd.* of Reading in 1947 when brewing ceased.

The market town of Alton has long associations with the brewing industry as the fertile surrounding area provides hops and barley. *Watney's Brewery* was a large complex in Turk Street dating mainly from the late 19th century although the original brewery was established in 1763. Brewing ceased in 1970 and the buildings were demolished; Sainsbury's supermarket now occupies the site. The logo on public house signs of *Watney's* contained a red barrel.

The original brewery of *Courage,* also located in Turk Street, consisted of a group of buildings dating from the 1880s to the 1960s but these were demolished in the 1970s. New premises were erected which incorporated a structure, squarely built of concrete and glass, in the late 1960s that belonged to *Harp Lager Brewery.* It is still in use today. See "Present breweries" for more details.

The original *Courage* brewery was founded by John Courage, a shipping agent from Aberdeen, who bought a brewhouse in Southwark, London in 1787 but it wasn't until 1903, after the business had been registered as a limited liability company in April 1888 that it acquired *Alton Brewery Co.* and 77 licensed houses. In 1955 *Courage* merged with *Barclay Perkins & Co. Ltd.* of Southwark, becoming *Courage & Barclay Ltd.* After further mergers and acquisitions the brewery transferred to Reading in 1979 where the company, still brewing beer, belongs to *Scottish & Newcastle UK.* The logo on signs of *Courage's* public houses was a cockerel with the words "take Courage".

Present breweries

Courage's plant at Alton is now operated by *Coors Brewers Ltd.* and named, appropriately, *Coors Brewery.* Founded by pioneering families and tracing its roots back to 1786, the company, along with its parent company, *Molson Coors Brewing Company,* have 18 breweries worldwide and over 40 brands of beer including Molson Canadian, Coors Light and Carling. The company also operates a brewery at Burton upon Trent where brewing is believed to date back to 1002 when Benedictine monks discovered that local well water produced superior stong ales!

After nearly 160 years *Gales Brewery* of Horndean changed hands in 2005 but how did this famous Hampshire brewery start? Richard Gale, born 1802, acquired *The Ship & Bell Inn* at Horndean in 1847, which was already renowned for its beer. In 1853 Richard's son, George, was running the pub that had its own brewery and within a short time he decided the potential for expansion was considerable. A fire destroyed the first brewery but a new one was built in 1869, mainly using the remains of the old one. Much of the new plant, including the brewing tower, forms the premises that are there today.

George Gale continued to expand his brewery business until 1888 when he registered it as a limited liability company. In 1896 he sold his major shareholding interest and chairmanship to Herbert Frederick Bowyer, a miller from Guildford, and his family ran the independent brewery until November 2005 when it was sold to *Fuller Smith & Turner* of *The Griffin Brewery,* Chiswick, West London, another family-owned brewery founded in 1846, the year before *Gales.* This brewery belongs to The Independent Family Brewers of Britain. *Gales* brands of beer include HSB (Horndean Special Bitter), Butser Bitter and Prize Old Ale. They were also known for their locally-produced cask beer. Among the brewery's achievement in awards are Regional Brewer of the Year 2001, and again in 2004 and 2005. The *Gales Brewery* flag was lowered for the last time on 31 March 2006 when *Fuller's* decided to close the Horndean site for brewing, transferring the brewing of ales such as HSB, Butser Bitter and Prize Old Ale to its Chiswick Brewery. The site is scheduled for redevelopment in the future.

Situated on the western edge of the New Forest at a crossing-point of the River Avon lies the small market town of Ringwood, steeped in history dating back to before the Domesday Book (1086). Four breweries and their maltings were recorded here in the early 1800s and one of these was owned by Stephen Tunks, a local banker, whose brewery stood on the site of the present day *Ringwood Brewery* in Christchurch Road. Only one brewery survived into the 20th century and that closed in 1923. There was to be a lapse of 55 years before the tradition of brewing resumed in 1978 with the establishment of *Ringwood Brewery* whose founder-members were Peter Austin and David Welsh. Special brands of beer include Old Thumper, Bold Forester, Fortyniner and Best Bitter. In 2005 the brewery won two awards – Bronze Medal for Best Bitter in the Munich Festival and in "The 100 small best companies to work for", organised by *The Times* newspaper, the brewery was placed 35th.

Romsey, another market town by the River Test, is famous for three buildings; the Abbey, founded in AD907 by Edward, son of Alfred the Great, "Broadlands", the 18th-century house, where Lord Palmerston, the Victorian Prime Minister (1855-8), was brought up, and later the home of Lord Mountbatten of Burma and finally *Strong's Brewery* at Horsefair. As previously mentioned this site has now been redeveloped but the brewing industry in the town is thriving on the Industrial Estate at Greatbridge Road by *Hampshire Brewery.* Founded in 1992 by Steve Windes, it operates as a limited company and moved to the present site in September 1997. To celebrate the occasion a new brew, Pride of Romsey, was created. In April 1999 *Hampshire Brewery* relaunched

Strong's Best Bitter to much local acclaim. Other brews associated with noble Kings of England include King Alfred's, Lionheart, Ironside, Pendragon and 1066. The brewery has won several awards over the years including the Gold Medal in the IBIA category for Strong Ales as well as Hampshire Beer of the Year in April 2000.

The *Flower Pots* is the only public house in the pretty village of Cheriton, which is best remembered for the decisive battle during the Civil War in 1644, but a short distance away is a purpose-built brewhouse founded in March 1993 by Ray Page, Jo Bartlett, Paul Tickner and Martin Roberts. The *Cheriton Brewhouse* produced traditional beers which included Diggers Gold, Pots Ale and Cheriton Best. In 1995 it won a Silver Medal in the Champion Beer Festival of Britain. However the original partnership ceased at the end of April 2006 and the brewhouse has now been renamed *Flower Pots Brewery.*

A few miles away, along the B3046 from Cheriton, we come to the quaint but beautiful town of New Alresford, famous for its watercress beds and the headquarters of the Mid-Hants Railway, known as "The Watercress Line". Not far away in Prospect Road is *Itchen Valley Brewery* established in 1997 by Simon Brown, who when attending a christening the same year as a godfather, decided that his first brewed beer should be called by that name! This brand went on to win an award at the Great British Beer Festival the same year. The following year the brewery won the Best Beer of Britain Bronze Medal at Olympia, the country's most prestigious Beer Festival. The range of hand-crafted beers produced by the brewery include, as well as Godfathers, Wykehams Glory (named after the 14th-century Bishop of Winchester), Fagins (the character from Charles Dickens' *Oliver Twist*), Dickens having been born at Portsmouth in 1812, and Pure Gold. The Hampshire Rose blend was introduced on the opening of the Rose Bowl, Southampton in 2002.

Whilst in this locality we proceed along the A31 from New Alresford to the village of Four Marks where *Triple "fff" Brewing Co. Ltd.* is based at Station Approach, the village also being on the Watercress Line. Founded in 1997 by Graham Trott at Four Marks, the name *Triple "fff"* derives from a musical term for loudness (dictionary definition: "of musical time having three beats in each bar"). The brands of beer are therefore taken from popular songs such as Stairway, Moondance and Little Red Rooster (The Rolling Stones). The brewery also produces Alton's Pride, a golden brown bitter, and new brands called Gilbert White, named after the clergyman and naturalist (1720-93), Rock Lobster and Crazy Diamond, in memory of the late Syd Barrett, founder member of Pink Floyd. In August 2006 the brewery won Bronze overall medal and Silver medal (Best Bitter category) at the Great British Beer Festival for Moondance.

The Oakleaf Brewing Co. Ltd. is a family-run brewery based at Clarence Wharf Industrial Estate, Gosport, founded in March 2000 by Dave Pickersgill and his son-in-law Ed Anderson. The company produced its first brew in December of the same year and has achieved various awards over the years including the Mild Gold Award for the SIBA National Competition 2004. Among the brands of beer they produce are Hole Hearted, one of their original ales, Blake's Gosport Bitter and Oakleaf Bitter.

The company also brews the beer made from barley grown on nearby Ports Down by Martin Bazeley, a farmer turned beer impresario, who operates *Southwick Brewhouse* in partnership with Al Stringer of Selborne.

The village of Southwick near Fareham is famous for its connection with the planning of the D-Day invasion of France on 6 June 1944 (code name Operation Overlord). Southwick House was requisitioned by the Royal Navy in 1940 and here General Dwight D. Eisenhower set up his forward headquarters with General Bernard Montgomery and other senior Allied Commanders.

The Brewhouse, a scheduled ancient monument, is situated in the yard at the rear of *The Golden Lion* public house whose history can be traced from the 17th century. Activity at the early Victorian brewhouse ceased in 1957 when the last master brewer, Dick Olding, retired. In 1985 the building and equipment, including the mash tun and the 145-year old horizontal steam engine and pump, were restored in a project co-ordinated by Southampton University Archaeology Group and Hampshire Historic Buildings Preservation Trust.

16. *Southwick Brewhouse* Southwick   *Photo: Southwick Brewhouse*

Martin Bazeley reopened the historic brewhouse in October 2005 as a beer and cider retail emporium along with his partner Al Stringer. The special brand of beer, Suthwyk Ales, is taken from the barley grown on Martin's farm and brewed by *The Oakleaf Brewing Co. Ltd.* as previously mentioned. The logo for *Southwick Brewhouse* incorporates the image of Dick Olding in the mash tun. The brewhouse includes a museum which contains old implements associated with the original building and presents a fascinating example of a Victorian domestic brewery, a rare survival of a once common establishment.

The Golden Lion's claim to fame? This is where Generals Eisenhower and Montgomery took sustenance as they planned the D-Day landings in June 1944, normally from the comfort of Lloyd Loom chairs!

White Star Brewery, based at Clewers Lane, Waltham Chase, was Southampton's first commercial brewery for over 50 years. Founded by brothers Andy and Chris Ingram in 2003, the initial two beers produced, Majestic and Capstan, won awards in the Eastleigh Beer Festival of the same year. Six regular brands are now brewed on the premises.

Finally, *The Winchester Brewery* is not based at Winchester, as one would expect, but in Southampton. The original plan was to re-introduce a brewery in our city but negotiations failed to materialize and so we find the brewery now operating from Longbridge Industrial Park, Northam, Southampton. It was formed in the last quarter of 2004 and formally launched in January 2005 with brewing commencing two months later. Founder member brewer David Wealleans teamed up with Phil Ambrose and their initial brews comprised two beers, recipes for which were developed before they even had a plant! These were Best Bitter and Trusty Servant. *The Winchester Brewery* is dedicated to the ancient capital of England and their aim is simply to provide beers with flavour that people like to drink – a good note on which to finish this chapter!

CHAPTER 6
The hotels – past and present

So that there is no confusion over the word "hotel" this chapter refers only to the buildings used solely for the purpose of commercially-run establishments providing the required accommodation which did or still do exist in the city.

Some licensed premises incorporating a small number of bedrooms are classified as hotels but these mainly operate as public houses and are therefore listed in chapter 8.

I have divided this chapter into two parts – the hotels of the past and those which are functioning at the present time. Firstly, I set out the hotels that are no longer in existence.

Past hotels

The *White Hart Hotel* closed in 1857 caused by the end of the coaching era but where was it? So many people pass by these buildings in High Street every day and fail to appreciate their fine architecture. I refer to Nos. 46, 47 and 48 High Street which now comprise the two shops occupied by British Bookshops:Sussex Stationers, JJB Sports and the small section of Lloyds TSB with the wooden-framed frontage. The great window with the centre Ionic column and balcony is a prominent feature of the main building which commenced as a hotel in 1806, the first proprietor being John Bell. The balcony was a favourite place for appearances by politicians addressing the public on the occasions of seeking votes for parliamentary elections. The Duke of Wellington, whilst staying at the hotel in 1852, spoke to the citizens from the balcony, which is still there today. The premises were sold in 1857 to Charles Sherry, the landlord of the *Black Swan Hotel,* who converted the ground floors into three shops. The present frontages to the two existing shops were installed in 1912. For many years the occupiers of the shops were Teague & King, music salon, (British Bookshops), Cliftons Ltd., outfitters, (JJB Sports) and John Kaines Ltd., pork butchers, (section of Lloyds TSB). The main building of Lloyds TSB, originally built in 1711 as the Guildhall, was converted into a draper's shop known as King & Son. The façade of the premises was remodelled by Thomas Stopher Junr. in 1914 for Lloyds Bank which opened the following year.

On the opposite side of High Street stands The House of God Begot. This is one of the most famous landmarks in Winchester, the present building dating from the 15th century although the original manor can be traced back to 1052 when Queen Emma, mother of Edward the Confessor, bequeathed the Manor of God Begot to the Priory of St. Swithun, which was situated where Symonds Street is today. Incidentally, Emma became the wife of two successive Kings of England, Ethelred, and following his death, she married Canute. After the Reformation the manor became the property of the Dean and Chapter of Winchester Cathedral and remained so until 1866 when

17. *God Begot House*, High Street. The present building dates from the 15th century. Converted into *God Begot Hotel* c.1866 and remained in that use until 1970.   *Photo: Author*

18. *The George Hotel* stood on the corner of High Street and Jewry Street. Rebuilt in 1769 as a coaching inn it closed in 1939, then used by the Ministry of Agriculture. Photo taken in 1955 before demolition the following year. Barclays Bank stands on the site today.
Photo: E.A. Sollars (Winchester Museums, Winchester City Council)

19. The rear of *The George Hotel*, St. George's Street. Note the covered pedestrian walkway from The George Garage (formerly stables) to the Hotel. *The City Tavern*, Jewry Street, is visible in the photo which was taken in March 1956 during demolition of the hotel.

Photo: E.A. Sollars (Winchester Museums, Winchester City Council)

it was sold and converted into a hotel known as *God Begot Hotel*. The premises became popular, especially with American tourists, who were able to stay in bedrooms with such names as Queen Emma and King Stephen, the son of William the Conqueror's daughter Adela. The ground floor of the building was converted into shop premises in the 1950s occupied by Bernfeld Ltd., antique jewellers and silversmiths, whilst the upper floor continued to be used as a hotel until 1970. By a strange coincidence, the licensee of the hotel in the 1950s was a John Bell, the same name as the first proprietor of The *White Hart Hotel,* 150 years previous! Eventually, the whole of the property was converted into a restaurant, firstly known by the name of Richoux and now called Ask Pizza-pasta. The name God Begot derives its curious name from the area on which the building stands, known from the 11th century as "God begeaton" meaning "good bargain".

Further up High Street on the corner of Jewry Street stood *The George Hotel,* a very popular venue in the 19th century. There had been an inn on the site since 1408 called *The Moon;* it was renamed *The George* in 1415 after King Henry V's battle-cry at the Battle of Agincourt. Rebuilt in 1769 as a coaching inn, the landmark was the covered pedestrian walkway which stretched across St. George's Street from the inn to the stables and coachmen's accommodation on the opposite side of the street. The bridge enabled ladies to walk from the hotel to the carriages (or vice-versa) avoiding their long dresses from being dragged through the muddy lane – St. George's Street being very narrow until 1956. An interesting feature of the hotel was the spacious winter-garden with its exotic plants and shrubs. The stables, approximately where Toni & Guy's hair salon is today, became The George Garage and the coachmen's accommodation was transformed into a residential flat, with six large rooms all partitioned off by wood panels, known as The George Garage Flat. My wife and I started our married life there in 1952 paying 15/6d. (77p) per week for the unfurnished flat. The stalls which housed the horses became the area where the local undertaker's hearse and mourners' cars were parked! Petrol pumps were situated underneath the flat; no wonder we could never obtain fire insurance for our furniture!

The hotel closed in 1939 and was bought by the Ministry of Transport who leased it to the Ministry of Agriculture as the county's headquarters of the Hampshire War Agricultural Executive Committee until demolition took place in 1956 for the purposes of widening Jewry Street and St. George's Street plus the erection of the new Barclays Bank, which opened on 9 February 1959. Previously the bank, the smallest in the city, was situated next to Kingdon & Co. Ltd., ironmongers, (now Waterstones). *The George Tap*, part of the hotel, stood at the rear on the corner of St. George's Street and Jewry Street.

The *Black Swan Hotel,* dating from 1700/3 and situated on the corner of High Street and Southgate Street was, before the main line railway opened in 1839, the principal stopping place for the old road wagons, four of which brought all the heavy goods in and out of the city. The hotel was managed by the aforementioned Charles Sherry in the 1850s; he is reputed to be the first licensee in Winchester to sell whisky and according to the notes of Thomas Stopher Junr. "a shocking strong tasting stuff it was, smoky and fiery; gin and brandy were the drinks generally used". Thomas wrote of Charles Sherry "He was an active, industrious little man with a short temper and given to upset his customers".

The wall of the premises on the St. Clement Street side contained the words "The Black Swan Hotel – motor garage with entrance – High Street"; the wall also contained a board advertising Savage & Weller's St. Clement Street sale rooms. On one of the chimney stacks the words "Black Swan Hotel" were painted.

But perhaps the hotel's chief claim to fame was that Sherlock Holmes, the famous detective created by Sir Arthur Conan Doyle, and his companion Dr. Watson, stayed at the hotel whilst engaged on the case of *The Copper Beeches.* As Holmes said "...An inn of good repute in the High Street, at no distance from the railway station and there we found the young lady waiting for us". They interviewed Miss Violet Hunter, who had contacted them earlier about rather "unusual requests" made on her by her employer, Jephro Runcastle. Thereafter Holmes and Watson journeyed to the house which "laid 5 miles on the far side of Winchester". All these facts are disclosed in the story *The Adventure of The Copper Beeches.* The village is thought to be Otterbourne and the house "Elderfield", originally the home of Charlotte Yonge, the 19th-century novelist and writer of children's books.

The Winchester Lodge of Economy of Freemasons No. 76. met in a large room over the hotel from 1854 to 1934 when the Lodge moved to the Masonic Hall on the corner of Parchment Street and St. George's Street (now part of W.H.Smith) and formerly a Wesleyan Chapel.

20. The *Black Swan Hotel* stood on the corner of High Street and Southgate Street. Dating from 1702/3 it was demolished in 1934 to make way for the widening of Southgate Street. The Black Swan Buildings occupy the site today.　　*Photo: Hampshire County Library*

The famous statue of The Black Swan was on the High Street side of the building, demolished in 1934 to make way for the widening of Southgate Street, the erection of The Black Swan Buildings and the installation of the first traffic-lights in the city. Before 1934 policemen, in white jackets, stood on rubber mats in the middle of the High Street junctions with Southgate Street and Jewry Street, directing the traffic. The replica of The Black Swan as seen today above Purple Picture Gallery shop was carved by Edwin Laverty, a craftsman in wood, who with his brother had their workshop at the lower end of St. Swithun Street, close by the church. The *Black Swan Tap* was not part of the hotel, as usually happened with "taps" adjoining breweries and hotels, but situated on the opposite side of Southgate Street at No.1a, now Blues Fresh Food for Thought takeaways. The Tap closed in 1923.

Ascending High Street we come to Moss Bros., menswear stores, formerly Basticks, outfitters, but this building on the corner of Trafalgar Street and High Street was one of the temperance hotels of the city and known from 1897 as *YMCA Temperance Hotel.* In 1923 the property became The Ladies County Club before conversion into shop premises in the late 1940s or early 1950s.

On the opposite side of High Street stand two fashion shops, Long Tall Sally and Pavilion, a clothing boutique, which was *The Westgate Lodge Hotel* from 1927 to 1970. Later the premises became the first Chinese restaurant in Winchester.

Parchment Street possessed two hotels, *Wykeham Temperence Hotel* operating from No. 11, was in existence from 1912 to 1929. People Like Us (House Furnishings) occupy the premises on the site today. Close by came *Essex Private Hotel* and, just inside the entrance to the cul-de-sac, was the GFS Hall (Girls' Friendly Society). The hotel, serving the community from 1925 to 1950, has now been converted into a private residence.

Winton Court Hotel occupied Nos. 47/49 Southgate Street, opposite the Screen Cinema, in the 1970s. The properties are now known as Devenish House for the Frail owned by St. John's & Allied Charities.

Entering St. Cross Road on the left-hand side, the private residence at No. 17, formerly the home and surgery of Dr. P.M. Oxley, was converted into *Oriel House Hotel* in 1951 and continued to be used as such until the late 1970s. A malt-house stood close by.

The distinctive building on the corner of St. Cross Road and Norman Road was known as *Norman Mede Hotel* from 1926 to 1960 when the name changed to *The Winchester Hotel*. The premises were converted into residential apartments in the 1980s and are now known as Forder Court. The garage associated with the hotel formerly known as The Reliance, is still in use today called Winchester Motor Company.

A short-lived hotel, erected as a private dwelling at the turn of the 20th century, situated on the corner of St. Cross Road and Barnes Close, was *St. Cross Hotel*. It is now a dental surgery known as St. Lawrence House Dental Practice.

Returning to the city centre, there is a fine row of late-Georgian houses at the far end of Tower Street coming from High Street, and No. 63. was, for a short while, converted into a hotel known as *The Portland;* this has now been converted back to a private residence.

Coming round "The Five Corners", now reduced to three, to the junction of Tower Street with Jewry Street, is the Theatre Royal but the front elevation and part of the side, at present coloured yellow, was built in 1850 as the *Market Hotel* by one Vaughn "a scamping, speculative builder who ran the hotel when it first opened" according to the notes of Thomas Stopher Junr. Vaughn also erected the adjoining premises stretching round into City Road. The main purpose of the hotel was to accommodate the farming community when attending the cattle-market and The Corn Exchange in Jewry Street. On the Tower Street side wall of the hotel were the words "Market Hotel – Welsh & Co. Ltd. celebrated ales, wines and spirits" which continued with the words "Headquarters C.T.C & N.C.U." (Cyclists Touring Club and National Cyclists Union). The hotel closed in 1912 and was purchased by John and James Simpkins who, utilising the yard at the rear, erected the auditorium, fly-tower and stage, thus converting the building into a cine-variety theatre, which opened on 24 August 1914 as the Theatre Royal. The Corn Exchange, after other uses, became the lending library in October 1936 and the cattle-market was turned into a car-park the same year. The whole complex has now been refurbished and extended into a "discovery centre" which opened on 27 November 2007. The Headquarters of C.T.C and N.C.U. transferred to the Jewry Tea Rooms next to the Criterion Restaurant, now Loch Fyne Fish Restaurant, Jewry Street, after the *Market Hotel* closed.

The *Theatre Bar,* on the corner of Tower Street and Jewry Street, was part of the hotel, first known as *The Market Inn,* then as *Theatre Bar* and finally *Theatre Pub.* The

21. The *Market Hotel*, on the corner of Jewry Street and Tower Street. Built in 1850 it continued to be used as a hotel until 1912. The front elevation and part of the side was converted into a cine-variety theatre in 1914. Now forms part of the frontage to the Theatre Royal. Photo taken c.1907. *Photo: Edward Roberts Collection (Hampshire Record Office)*

22. The *Carfax Hotel*, on the corner of Sussex Street and Station Hill. Saunders cycle shop was converted to a hotel in 1918 which continued until 1967. Photo taken in 1973 shortly before demolition. Hampshire Record Office occupies the site today.

Photo: Winchester Museums, Winchester City Council

licence continued until the theatre closed in January 1996 for extensive refurbishment. The original bar is now incorporated into the theatre, known as the *Denplan Stalls Bar*, and is used solely by patrons attending shows at the theatre or for other functions organized by the management.

Around the corner in City Road, the premises now occupied at No. 25 by Hampshire County Youth Service was originally called Oriel House but in 1899 the premises were converted into *Oriel Temperance Hotel* which continued to be used as such until 1934. A large board on the side flint wall advertised live shows and films at the Theatre Royal. According to the street directory the Simpkins brothers had control of the hotel at some time during its 35 years usage as a hotel – hence the board.

Not far away at No. 1 Station Hill stood another temperance hotel known from 1897 as *Turner's Temperance Hotel*, renamed *Sharp's Temperance Hotel* in 1917, which continued to exist under this name until 1928.

On the corner of Station Hill and Sussex Street stood Saunders cycle shop which was converted to the *Carfax Hotel* in 1918. After the closure of *Sharp's Temperance Hotel* in 1928 the proprietors of the *Carfax* took over the premises in 1929 and extended their hotel into Nos. 1 and 2 Station Hill. The name *Carfax* comes from old French "carrefures" meaning the "meeting of roads". Here we have six roads converging at one point – Sussex Street, Station Hill, Stockbridge Road, Andover Road, Swan Lane and City Road.

The premises ceased to be a hotel in 1967 and was then used as a hostel for students of King Alfred College (now University of Winchester). The property then became "digs for diggers", students who flocked to excavate old Winchester during the summer months. It closed altogether in 1972 and was demolished the following year, the site only to lay empty for two full decades before being acquired by Hampshire County Council to make way for the new Hampshire Record Office which was opened by HM the Queen on 19 November 1993.

On the corner of Andover Road and Swan Lane stands Eagle Court. This was built c.1848 as the *Eagle Hotel*, the first property to be erected in this area. For many years the late Gordon Holland was proprietor of the hotel, whose family had associations with that area over a long period of time as motor engineers on the site now occupied by Richard Steel & Partners, funeral directors. The hotel was converted into residential flats in 2001.

From Swan Lane we turn into Hyde Street where visitors to Winchester in the 1950s could get slightly confused, Hyde Street having two hotels close to one another with practically the same name – *Hyde Abbey Hotel* at No. 21a, now numbered 22, and *Hyde Abbey House Private Hotel and Restaurant* at No.23. Sandwiched in between these two buildings is Hyde Street Chapel, formerly Evangelical Free Church. I have dealt with *Hyde Abbey Hotel* in section XVI of chapter 8 as this was more a pub than a hotel.

Hyde Abbey House, built in the middle of the 17th century, with a new front erected in the 18th century, gives the property its present Queen Anne appearance. The building became a private school for boys, founded in about 1760 by Revd Rynell

23. *Hyde Abbey House Hotel*, Hyde Street. Built in mid-17th century, the property became a private school for boys c.1760. From 1950 to c.1975 it became a private hotel and restaurant. Now occupied by Pierre Fabre as their administration office.   *Photo: Author*

Cotton, the annual school fees being £31! On Cotton's death in 1779 the school passed into the hands of his son-in-law Revd Charles Richards, who combined the duties of schoolmaster with his position as Rector of the 12th-century church of St. Bartholomew, Hyde. The school was recognised as one of the finest classical schools in the kingdom; George Canning (1770-1827), British statesman and briefly Prime Minister, was educated at the school which closed in 1833 on the death of Charles Richards.

However from 1950 to c. 1975 the property became a private hotel and restaurant; it is now occupied by Pierre Fabre, the administration office of a French pharmaceutical company.

A short distance up Sussex Street and on the corner of Gladstone Street stood *Cowdray Lodge Hotel* which was demolished in 1973 to make way for the widening of Gladstone Street and the redevelopment of that area which now incorporates Gladstone car-park.

Branching into Bereweeke Road from Stockbridge Road and opposite Bereweeke Avenue stands a property now converted into flats for Eastleigh Housing Association. This was built in 1903 as a private house, later becoming Finlay House Nursing Home. From c.1964 to the late 1990s it was the *Chantry Mead Hotel.*

Continuing along Stockbridge Road we come to an area formerly known as the farming district of Wyke, now called Weeke, and close to the little Norman church of St. Matthew stood a small guest-house called *The Travellers Rest.* Part of the property has now been converted into a private dwelling known as "Crispin Cottage", while the rest was demolished to form a cul-de-sac called Travellers End.

To complete the story of the city's past hotels I come back into the heart of Winchester and finish my journey with a building that stands on the corner of Eastgate Street and Bridge Street, now known as Eastgate House and occupied by Smiths Gore, chartered surveyors. This was originally the *Eastgate Hotel,* opened in 1902 and for many years the licensee was Charles Salter. It closed as a hotel in the 1980s. I relate the history of the original Eastgate House in chapter 8 – section I.

Present hotels

I start at the lower end of the city with *The Wessex Hotel.* In 1960 the City Council approved plans "in principle" for the erection of a new hotel by Trust Houses Ltd. on the site of the cathedral car-park and spreading across Paternoster Row into Colebrook Street. Proposals for the hotel were put forward in conjunction with the Dean and Chapter of the cathedral because the site was an ancient burial ground and Parliamentary sanction had to be obtained. Consultations were also made with The Winchester Preservation Trust (now The City of Wnchester Trust) who were concerned as to the precise location of the hotel. Local residents were also unhappy in having a modern building so close to the Norman cathedral. A "Letter to the Editor" of the *Hampshire Chronicle* stated: "If the hotel is built the house of God will be quite shut in and only patrons of the hotel will be able to see and get near the cathedral <u>without a long walk</u>".

However, detailed plans were finally approved and the hotel took two years to build costing £600,000. Named *The Wessex Hotel* it opened on 15 February 1964 and was described by the *Hampshire Chronicle* as a "modern concept in the lee of the cathedral".

24. *The Mercure Wessex Hotel,* on the corner of Market Lane and Colebrook Street, built on the site of an ancient burial ground, opened on 15 February 1964. The postal address is Paternoster Row which now passes underneath the hotel.   *Photo: Author*

Some flint work embedded in the elevations of the hotel comes from the original flint wall of the car-park. In the forecourt, under the pillars, are the words Amen Court referring to Amen Passage which was close by. The complex started as a *Trust House Forte* hotel but is now known as *Mercure Wessex Hotel.*

25. *The Winchester Royal Hotel*, St. Peter Street. Built in the reign of King Charles II, and once used as a convent for refugee English Benedictine nuns, was converted into a hotel in 1858.   *Photo: Author*

The oldest surviving hotel of the city is to be found in St. Peter Street. The *Royal Hotel,* built in the reign of King Charles II, was once known as The Bishop House. It incorporates part of the Tudor House of Lady Mary West erected on land owned by Wherwell Priory and was a "Secret Centre" for local Catholics in the 1580s. Following the sale to the Catholic London District, the property became a convent for refugee English Benedictine nuns in 1794, and was converted to a hotel in 1858. Now known as *The Winchester Royal Hotel* it belongs to the *Forestdale* chain of hotels based at Lyndhurst.

A short distance along Southgate Street stands *Hotel du Vin.* Built in 1715 as a private house, with a garden and stables, possibly for John Littlehales, an eminent doctor, it became the home of the Crawford family from 1868 to 1928 when the property was purchased by David Hatchwell who converted the building into a private hotel which opened in 1929 as the *Southgate Hotel.* By 1935 the stables area had been demolished and a major extension was added to the original premises with further additions made in 1997. From the mid-1930s to the 1950s the offices of the English Speaking Union were contained within the hotel which was taken over by Catering Houses Ltd. in 1952/3. The name changed to *Hotel du Vin* in October 1994 and since then it has belonged to the *MWB Ltd.* chain of hotels.

26. *Hotel du Vin*, Southgate Street. Built in 1715 as a private house, it was converted into a hotel in 1928, opening the following year as *Southgate Hotel*. The name changed to *Hotel du Vin* in 1994.   *Photo: Author*

During the Second World War General Montgomery (later Viscount Montgomery of Alamein) dined there when visiting his son, David, who was a scholar at Winchester College. Sir Anthony Eden, when Prime Minister, also dined there.

Built in 1890 as a private residence, No. 50 Christchurch Road was converted to a bed and breakfast outlet c.1980 and called *No. 50*. In 2000 the premises reopened, after extensive refurbishment, as *Giffard House Hotel,* named after the second Norman Bishop of Winchester, William Giffard (1100-1129).

On the outskirts of the city along Harestock Road we come to *Harestock Lodge Hotel,* built as a private house in the 1870s. This was the home of the Commander of the Light Infantry based at Peninsula Barracks. The property was converted into a bed and breakfast outlet c.1978 and eventually expanded into a private hotel.

Finally, we come back into the city to Worthy Lane, where a new coach station built at the cost of £7700 was opened on 1 June 1934. This served as a pick-up/drop-off point for coaches travelling to and from London and going further afield to or coming from Bournemouth and the West country. The "Royal Blue" coaches, along with others from various companies, were authorized to use the new facility which could accommodate 34 coaches at a time. The house known as "Hyde Lodge" immediately adjoining the station was converted to a waiting-hall, booking office and a restaurant, later to be known as Beech Tree Café. In 1938 the city council sold a plot of land adjacent to the coach station to *Eldridge Pope & Co. Ltd.* for £250 for the building of a hotel which opened the following year as *Coach Station Hotel.* Provision was made for *Eldridge Pope* to erect "signs on the bank of each of the two entrances to the coach station" to advertise their hotel. When the coach station finally closed in about 1980, the hotel was extended and became *Saxon Hotel* in 1985, the name changing again in 1990 to *Winchester Moat House Hotel.*

Since 2004 the hotel has belonged to *Pedersen Hotels* who totally refurbished their new acquisition in 2006, renaming the premises *The Winchester Hotel,* taking the place of the hotel by the same name which existed in St. Cross Road. The coach station area is now used by guests of the hotel and for the parking of coaches on day visits by tourists to the city from different parts of the country and abroad.

A new hotel, yet to be built, is proposed on a site by the roundabout adjacent to the Intech Science & Discovery Centre.

27. *The Winchester Hotel,* Worthy Lane, opened in 1939 as *Coach Station Hotel* being an addition to the coach station which had been operating since 1 June 1934.

Photo: Author

CHAPTER 7
A Ramble through the Ancient City

An anonymous author produced a story, possibly in the early 1900s, connecting all the pubs in Winchester, although a few hotels also appear such as the *George, Eagle* and *Market.* It is, however, a remarkable composition.

The next chapter deals with all the public houses included in the story together with some additional ones which existed before the author put pen to paper! Here, then, is the story.

Strolling into Winchester one morning, in the company of my friend *Hyde,* we saw a *Roebuck* watching an *Old Red Deer,* and when we got to the *Railway,* we heard the report of a rifle by a *Volunteer,* which startled a *Fox and Hounds,* and by the light of the *Morning Star,* we saw the *Fox* run past the *Monument* and was killed trying to get under the *Westgate.* I then discovered by the light of the *Star* that my friend was wearing a *Plume of Feathers* plucked from the wings of the *Black Swan* which was shot by a *Sportsman* under the *Willow Tree* which greatly annoyed the *Queen,* it being a *Royal* bird so we gave it to the *Duke of Edinburgh* who with *Perseverance* had obtained the services of the *Black Boy* who trained the *Golden Lion* to leap through the *King's Arms* and alight on the *Duke's Head* and ring a *Bell* and play with the *Dog and Duck* and set light to a *Catherine Wheel.* This was being performed in the *New Town Hall,* when who should we see but *Victoria* in the *Gladstone Arms* wearing a *Rose and Crown,* yes! a *Rose and Crown* on the *Queen's Head* seated on a *Crown and Cushion* riding on a *Coach and Horses* driven by a *Green Man* singing *Rule Britannia.* Three cheers for the *Red, White and Blue, John Barleycorn,* God bless the *Prince of Wales* etc. (which disturbed the *Poulterer's Rest* who was asleep at the *Fountain Head)* and the *Duke of Wellington,* the *Hero,* riding behind on a *Running Horse,* wearing the *Rose and Shamrock* followed by *George Shades* who had painted the *Indian Arms* on the *Royal Standard* and was going to fix it on the *Hampshire House* with a *Good Intent.* We then strolled past the *Post Office* and fell into the *City Wine Vaults* where we found several taps so we tried two *Brewery Taps* besides the *Queen's Brewery Tap, Water Lane Tap,* a *Railway Tap,* a *Lawn Tap,* a *Black Swan Tap,* and then we spotted a *Royal Tap* fixed into *Three Tuns* of good stuff, made from the grapes of the *Old Vine,* which had got into the *King's Head* and caused him to fall over the *Beehive* on the *Lawn,* and had to be taken to the *Guildhall* where they applied a *Battery* when in walked *Robin Hood* with a *Bird-in-Hand* who said he had just seen *St. James* and *St. John* in company with the *Cricketers* with a *Bat and Ball* going to play at the *Criterion,* and wanting fine weather, were looking at the *Rising Sun* which happened to be in the *Eclipse.* By this time a good company had arrived; some very fine men and had a little argument about who had the largest muscle, so we decided to measure the *Butcher's Arms, Baker's*

Arms, the *Mason's Arms,* the *Carpenter's Arms,* the *Skinner's Arms,* the *Coachmaker's Arms,* the two *Gardener's Arms,* the *Miller's Arms,* the *Mildmay Arms,* the *Wykeham Arms,* the *Fulflood Arms,* and all the *Forester's Arms';* in fact we measured the whole of the *City Arms* and *County Arms,* even the County of *Suffolk Arms,* but we found the most muscle in the *Blacksmith's Arms,* who shod three *White Horses* which we had purchased at the *Market* in *Sussex.* These were hooked to the *Plough* which was well handled by the *Jolly Farmer* who tilled the ground round the *Royal Oak* where he turned up an *Old Bell and Crown* but we made an *Exchange* for a *New Bell and Crown* which we placed on the *Nag's Head.* We next purchased a *Waggon and Horses* and loaded up the *Wheat Sheaves,* which was driven by *Albert* with a *3d. Whip* over the *Bridge* to the *Old Market* where we fell in with *Napoleon* who had been round the *Globe* in a *Ship* and had lost his *Crown and Anchor* and brought home an *Eagle* and a *Dolphin* and we laughed at him when he said he had his *Heart in Hand;* of course he meant the *White Hart.* He had brought home a *White Swan,* but had left his boy *George* taking a little *Railway Refreshment* at the *Great Western,* who if he ever entered an *Albion* or a *City Restaurant* or any *Wine Stores* or a *Railway Tavern* or a *New Inn,* was always noted to be *The First In and Last Out.* The night was now drawing on, and we thought we would like to stay in a *Winton Ale House,* so we settled down for the night in the *Old House at Home.*

Omega.

GOD SAVE THE KING

CHAPTER 8
The pubs – past and present

The final chapter, dealing with the city's public houses, has been divided into various sections depending in which part of Winchester they existed or are still functioning today, but firstly, you may like to know about the origin of our public houses.

This can be traced back to Roman times. Inns were common along the roads of Roman Britain, providing lodgings for officials and others travelling, sometimes, to inhospitable outposts of the empire. There were also small hut-like establishments – taberna – from which the word 'tavern' is derived. With the departure of the Romans from Britain, customer service really went downhill and it was not until the Middle Ages that things picked up as the monasteries created guest-houses and hospices to provide much of the available lodgings for travellers. Frequently the bread and ale was offered free at these venues.

Strictly speaking, inns provided rooms for travellers, taverns provided food and drink, while alehouses simply dished out beery substances. Since most of the population were illiterate it was quite common for each tavern or inn to display a simplistic sign which depicted the name of the alehouse. The concept of signage may have been imported by the Romans and one 15th-century manuscript describes an alehouse with an ivy bush sign hanging outside. Many of the signs which developed over the centuries were adapted from tradesman's signs – hence the *Baker's* or *Carpenter's Arms*. Doves were associated with monastic hostelries and a *Railway Arms* sign was close to railway stations.

With the gradual spread of the road network and horse-drawn coaches our roadside inns were transformed into coaching inns, such public houses even now preserving the archways which lead to former stables and courtyards behind – *The Old Coach House Inn* (now *Alfie's*) on the Broadway being a typical example.

SECTION I
From Bar End to Broadway

Entering Winchester from Park-and-Ride's St. Catherine's or Barfield the first pub we approach is The *Heart in Hand* standing on the corner of Milland Road, which was called New Road until 1927. This watering-hole is 200 years old and originally served refreshments to travellers bound for Portsmouth along the old Roman Road through Morestead and Owslebury. The premises, enlarged if not completely rebuilt in 1911, belonged to *Winchester Brewery* and *Marston's* before becoming a *Greene King* pub.

28. The *Heart in Hand*, on the corner of Bar End Road and Milland Road. The original pub, over 200 years old, served refreshments to travellers bound for Portsmouth along the old Roman Road through Morestead and Owslebury. Enlarged, if not completely rebuilt, in 1911.   *Photo: Author*

Travel further along Bar End Road and you arrive at a junction connecting Chesil Street with East Hill and Wharf Hill, the latter leading to Blackbridge Wharf situated at the north end of the Itchen Navigation. This canal transported mainly coal from Southampton Docks and closed in 1869 when the railways took over, but the bargees' cottages still exist in Wharf Hill and Domum Road. There are plans to reopen a section of the canal when sufficient funds are made available. At one time there were four pubs in the working-class district of Wharf Hill, all close to one another – now only one remains – the *Black Boy*.

A building has been on this site since 1750 trading as a public house for 200 years. Formerly belonging to *Whitbreads*, it was operated by *Courage* in the late 1970s. David Nicholson purchased the property in 1999, and so the *Black Boy* became one of the city's Free Houses and privately-owned pubs. The inn features a bizarre collection of century-old stuffed animals including a baboon in a kilt, two dogs, a badger, a fox and two crocodiles! The "hand-out card" states that the venue has been described as quirky or even eccentric in some pub guides, but that hides the true essence of the pub which is first and foremost a local boozer. In August 2006 plans were approved to build a two-storey bed-and-breakfast complex comprising four rooms with en-suite facilities and the enclosing of the garden to make a courtyard for customers. In October 2006 a scheme to provide an outside seating area at the watering-hole was also approved by the city planners.

Almost opposite on what is now a patch of green grass, stood *The Dog & Duck* which closed in 1923. The property remained empty until demolition took place in 1937.

29. The *Black Boy*, Wharf Hill, has been trading as a pub for 200 years. One of the city's Free Houses and privately-owned boozers. *Photo: Author*

It had a porch with simple plank seats where men drank in fine weather and children played in wet weather! On the outside wall were the words "Colson's Genuine Ales & Stout", supplied by *Chesil Brewery* referred to in chapter 3. This was, after all, a *Colson* pub!

There had been a mill at the foot of Wharf Hill since the 12th century, the present building dating from 1885. For many years R.G. Gifford Ltd., corn and coal merchants,

30. *The Dog & Duck*, Wharf Hill stood on what is now a patch of green grass, almost opposite the *Black Boy.* It closed in 1923 but was not demolished until 1937. Photo taken c.1897
Photo: George Roger Brown

operated the mill prior to S.C.A.T.S. taking over. Close to the mill and practically adjoining each other were two pubs, the *Duke's Head* (No.41) and *The Millers' Arms* (No.44). The former ceased trading in 1905 but between 1928 and 1941 the property was converted into a laundry known as Wharf Hill Hand Laundry while *The Millers' Arms* closed in 1924 and became a private house. The properties were eventually demolished to make way for the 1970 extension to the luxury apartments at Wharf Mill which had been converted for residential purposes at the same time by local builders Bendall Developments Ltd.

On the corner of Wharf Hill and Chesil Street stands *The King's Arms*. The building dates from c.1550 and has been a pub since c.1770. The boozer is practically opposite the *Black Boy* and in October 2006 David Nicholson purchased the property and so the venue became another privately-owned city pub. The long-term plan, however, was to convert the building into a restaurant, and this was achieved in June 2007 with the name changed to The Black Rat Restaurant. Prior to David's acquisition of the premises *The King's Arms* had been geared towards the "gay" community.

31. *The King's Arms*, on the corner of Wharf Hill and Chesil Street. The building dates from c.1550 and has been a pub since c.1770. Privately-owned since October 2006 and now The Black Rat Restuarant. *Photo: Author*

Not far away on the site now occupied by Weir Flats stood a pub called the *Duke of Edinburgh* named, not after our present Duke, but after Queen Victoria's second son (1844-1900) who became Duke of Saxe-Coburg-Gotha in 1893 as his paternal uncle's successor. The pub closed in 1923 and was occupied by *East Winchester Social Club,* a working men's club, until 1930 before conversion into part of Webb's butcher's shop.

Further down the street at No.63 was the *Good Intent* on which site now stands the extension to a private house known as "Mallard Cottage" (No.64). The property adjoins the passageway leading to Chesil Terrace where my mother was born in 1885. The licensed premises was a *Colson* pub, not far from *Chesil Brewery.* The pub, like the *Duke of Edinburgh,* ceased trading in 1923 and became a fried fish shop until 1930 when the building was demolished.

Just below the magnificent building known as "Kingsland House" is *East Winchester Social Club* (No.50) which moved down to these premises in 1930 and is still operating today. There are another four similar clubs in the city.

Opposite the entrance to Park-and-Ride's Chesil car-park is a cream-coloured house with a green front door (No.42). This was originally a pub called *The Railway Inn,* also known at one time as *Railway Tap.* Its connection with the Chesil railway on the other side of the street is the reason for the name. The licensed premises, at one time belonging to *Chesil (Colson's) Brewery,* was named after the Didcot, Newbury & Southampton Railway whose Winchester station, opening on 1 May 1885, was situated on the site now occupied by the Chesil multi-storey car-park. The pub closed in 1960 when the demise of the railway took place. Passenger traffic was withdrawn from the line in March 1960 but through freight trains to and from the Midlands continued until April 1964 when the line closed and the rail tracks were lifted. The name *The Railway Inn* was painted high on the front wall of the premises. From 1960 to 1964 Slape & Partners, Insurance and Mortgage Brokers, used the property as their offices before its transformation into a private residence.

There were two pubs in Winchester named the *Brewers Arms,* the site of the first one, practically opposite *Chesil Brewery,* and close to St. Peter's Church was formerly known as *The Drum* closed in 1913, converting to a private residence before demolition took place.

A short distance along St. John's Street stood *St. John's Tavern* (No.10) which closed in 1931 becoming a dwelling now conveted into flats. The marking on the front wall where the name of the pub used to be is still visible.

Perhaps the most famous, and believed to be the oldest surviving house in Winchester, is at the top of the street on the corner with Blue Ball Hill known as *The Blue Boar* which dates from c.1340. The property was at one time an inn which existed long before 1900 but it has such a fascinating history that I felt its story should be told and included in this chapter. The dwelling was originally known as *The White Boar,* the name of the personal badge of Richard III. The king was killed at the battle of Bosworth Field in 1485 by Henry VII who had been helped by a minor nobleman, the Earl of Oxford, and his badge was a Blue Boar; consequently all publicans with signs of the White Boar were quick to paint them blue. The watering-hole was known as *Blue Ball Inn* through the customary ignorance of the city council and the same applied to Blue Ball Hill which should have been called Blue <u>Boar</u> Hill.

It was 300 years after the *The White Boar* was built that the inn saw its most famous customer, when on a hot summer's day in 1764, a group of volunteer soldiers poured into the pub. The landlady couldn't have guessed at the time that one of these soldiers would have a military memorial stone in The Close of Winchester Cathedral. He was,

32. *The Blue Boar*, on the corner of St. John's Street and Blue Ball (Boar) Hill, is the oldest house in Winchester, dating from c.1340. At one time an inn, it is famous for its connection with Thomas Thetcher. Now a private residence. *Photo: Author*

after all, 26 years old, a private and not even a regular soldier but his "claim to fame" was to drink mild beer which killed him. Yet for every tourist who seeks the tomb of Field Marshal Wavell, buried in the cloisters of Winchester College, a dozen look for the grave of Thomas Thetcher. The tombstone reads:

"In memory of Thomas Thetcher, a Grenadier in the
North Regt. of Hants Milita who died of a violent
fever contracted by drinking small beer when hot.
12 May 1764 Aged 26 years"

On the memorial stone are these wise words:

"Soldiers be wise from his untimely fall,
And when ye're hot, drink Strong or none at all"

to which are added:

"An honest Soldier never is forgot
Whether he die by musket or by pot"

What became of the inn? The property fell into disrepair and in October 1966 it was hit by a jib belonging to Caswell Cranes of Winnall. However, the late Wilfred Carpenter Turner, a well-known Winchester architect, skilfully restored the dwelling a few years later and it was further refurbished in 1985 as a private residence. As far as I am aware, this historic house has no ghosts!

Ascending Morn Hill, on the right-hand side, is *The Rising Sun*, formerly a cellar house from Tudor times to the 18th century. The pub acquired the name of *The Rising Sun* because it was the most easterly inn of the city. Vandals from St. Giles's Fair, held annually on 1 September at St. Giles's Hill, were locked up in the police cellar. The ground floor of the cellar was, at one time, on the same level as the road outside the pub. On the front wall the words "May & Co. Ales & Stout – The Rising Sun" were painted. The Rising Sun is the Yorkist emblem of the "Sun in Splendour" – hence Shakespeare's *"Now is the winter of our discontent: made glorious Summer by this Sun of York"* – taken from *Richard III*, Act 1, Scene 1, line 1. At one time the pub belonged to *Courage*. It is now a Free House and the present lessee, Alfred Morrison, has been its landlord for the last 16 years.

33. *The Rising Sun*, Bridge Street, formerly a cellar house from Tudor times to the 18th century.   *Photo: Author*

Further along Alresford Road we come to *The Golden Lion*, built in 1932, to serve the Fairdown housing estate. It was a *Strong & Co. of Romsey Ltd.* pub but now belongs to *Wadworth* of Devizes. The licensed premises took the place of the original *Golden Lion* referred to in section XI of this chapter. Totally refurbished in 2006 the boozer is popular for its curry nights! A large beer-garden is situated at the rear of the venue.

The Post Office, which adjoined the pub, closed on 26 March 2003 and its postbox, originally in the courtyard of the Post Office, was relocated immediately in front of the pub sign in September 2003. The postbox (No. 231) is rare as it is the only one in Winchester which bears the marking "EviiiR". Edward VIII abdicated in 1936 before he was crowned King of Great Britain and Northern Ireland. There are only 132 of Type "B" postbox, of which the Alresford Road box is one, with this marking still being used in the country.

By the roundabout dividing the A31 and A272 is the original main road to Alresford which now leads to the Morn Hill Caravan Club site. Fronting this road is a pub, formerly known as *The New Inn*, but the name changed in 1982 to *The Percy Hobbs*. The plaque on the bar wall explains the reason thus: "Percy Hobbs, 1898-1983, local

34. *The Golden Lion*, Alresford Road. Note the postbox under the pub sign, the only one in Winchester which bears the marking "EviiiR". *Photo: Author*

farmworker, drank in this house for 63 years this being from 1920 when beer was 2 old pence a pint. In 1982 the house was renamed *The Percy Hobbs* in recognition of his loyalty". Framed photographs appear on the wall with Percy standing outside the pub under the original name of *The New Inn* and of him with his own pub sign. I inspected the tankard from which he drank; this is engraved "Percy Hobbs, 59 years regular customer *The New Inn*. Presented by Whitbreads 1979". The pub is now part of the *Brewers Fayre* chain belonging to *Mitchells & Butlers*.

35. *The Percy Hobbs*, by roundabout dividing the A31 and A272. Originally *The New Inn*, re-named in 1982 after its most regular customer "who drank in this house for 63 years".
Photo: Author

Returning to the Bridge Street corner of Water Lane we come to the *Blonde Beer Café* named after the Blond (sic) beer, Hoegaarden White, Grimbergen, Judas and Leffe beers originating from Belgium. The pub, formerly *The Cricketers' Arms,* belonged to *Courage*. It is now in the ownership of *Satbar Ltd.,* and was reopened on 2 February 2007 after a £40,000 upgrade.

At the rear of the *Blonde Beer Café* stood *The Bat and Ball,* very appropriate when the former was *The Cricketers' Arms.* Incorporated into *The Bat and Ball,* which closed in 1908, was the Penny Dinner Kitchen; this continued until 1926.

On the opposite side of Water Lane was the *Fox Inn* which stood close by the former Y.H.A. hostel. The pub closed c1954 and was demolished in 1958/59 as part of the plan for the creation of Riverside Walk.

36. *Blonde Beer Café*, Bridge Street, originally known as *The Cricketers' Arms.*   *Photo: Author*

In 1900 Wales Street was one of the "slum" areas of Winchester and has changed more than almost any other street in the city. This was very narrow and when redevelopment of the whole area took place in the 1960s the street was widened to its present width until reaching the pub *First In Last Out* which dates from the 17th century. Consequently the street narrows at this point to take in the pub. The adjoining cottage was amalgamated, many years ago, into the licensed premises which today belongs to the *Punch Tavern* chain but at one time it was a *Colson* pub with the *Winnall Brewery* almost adjoining it (see chapter 3). Why the name *First In Last Out?* It has nothing to do with going into the pub "first sober" and coming out "the last" in a "stupor"! In the days of coach and horses Easton Lane would have been the main road leading into Winchester from Alresford and the pub was the first stop for a drink before entering the city; likewise, it was the last one, for a "top-up", when leaving Winchester! With the "golden cockerel" still proudly displayed over the framework where a newly painted sign, depicting a racehorse first past "the post", is to be placed (see back cover), this is a clear indication that, over the years, the venue belonged to the *Courage* chain of pubs.

37. *First In Last Out*, Wales Street, dates from the 17th century . *Photo: Author*

Retracing our steps to the corner of Wales Street and Durngate we come to *The Ship Inn*. Originally two pubs stood next door to one another, *The Wheatsheaf* (No.4) and *The Ship Inn* (No.5). By 1910 only *The Wheatsheaf* remained and that changed its name in 1916 to *The Ship Inn* which is still trading today under the ownership of *Marston's PLC*. The present pub is in the same former combined building set in what was in 1900 a peaceful street, but since its redevelopment in the 1960s, has now become a busy thoroughfare for cars and lorries travelling to and from the Winnall Industrial Estate and Tesco's Supermarket!

38. *The Ship Inn*, Wales Street which was known as *The Wheatsheaf* until 1916. *Photo: Author*

On the opposite side of Water Lane in Bridge Street stood *The Bridge Inn* which closed in 1909 and was converted into Chisnell's garage in 1912. The site is now occupied by a row of four shops with living accommodation above.

Crossing over the road bridge we arrive at the pub now known as *The Bishop on the Bridge,* In the 1850s the site contained a dwelling-house and shop for which a licence was later granted under the name of *The Globe* (taking the place of the original *Globe,* demolished late 1860s, for the erection of the present Guildhall – see next section). Adjoining *The Globe* in Colebrook Street stood another pub called *The George & Dragon* (the postal address for both pubs was 1 & 2 Colebrook Street). These properties, purchased by *Eldridge Pope*, were demolished in 1891 and a new pub, built on the site at the cost of £1290, was opened in 1892 as *The Great Western Hotel* named after the railway which came to the lower end of Winchester in 1885. In its time the pub has been called by several names including *The Riverside Inn, The Louisiana, The Old Monk* and more recently *The Bishop on the Bridge.* This name refers to St. Swithun, the Saxon and 16th Bishop of Winchester from AD852 to 862. who built the first bridge over the fast-flowing River Itchen, the present bridge being constructed in 1813. James Cagney, the Hollywood actor, famous for portraying gangster roles in films, stayed at the pub in 1942 when he came to Winchester to visit American servicemen at St. Swithun's School, used during the war as a Red Cross Hospital. He also visited *Winchester Brewery* in Hyde Street, referred to in chapter 3. By way of interest, Bert Spicer, a well-known Winchester publican, operated only two licensed premises in his long career and both were connected with railways; *The Great Western* and *The Railway Tavern* in Station Hill (see section XV). He was for many years Chairman of the Winchester Licensed Victuallers Association. *The Bishop on the Bridge* is now owned by *Fuller Smith & Turner*

39. *The Bishop on the Bridge*, No.1 High Street. The present pub was built in 1891/2 and has been known by several names over the years.   *Photo: Author*

of Chiswick. The East Gate of the city stood approximately where the pub is today and was demolished in 1768.

The original Eastgate House dated from the late 17th-century, at the time when the building of the King's House for Charles II (designed by Sir Christopher Wren) was commenced but never finished and now forms part of Peninsula Square in Romsey Road. Eastgate House stood near the present junction of Eastgate Street with The Broadway. It was a large four-storey red-bricked building, overtopping all other houses in that area, according to Thomas Stopher Junr., who wrote many articles in the *Hampshire Chronicle* between 1897 and 1924. It had railings and iron gates in front of a carriage drive. The grounds at the rear of the house, generally referred to as "The Lawn", were long and narrow, tapering towards their northern extent to Durngate and bounded to the west by St. John's House and Buck Lane. In the centre of "The Lawn" was a narrow lake with a semi-circular end away from the house. The last occupier of Eastgate House was Lady Jane Mildmay who married Sir Henry Paulet St. John Bart., of Dogmersfield who took on the name of Mildmay, and so the house became known locally as Mildmay House. It was also sometimes referred to as Lawn House. After the death of her husband in 1808 the Dowager Lady Mildmay renewed the lease (the freehold of which belonged to Winchester College), every ten years the last time being in 1838. In 1844 the house and "The Lawn" was put up for auction and sold off in 46 freehold building lots. The house was demolished in 1846/47; the railings and gates were taken down and re-erected in front of "Kingsland House" in Chesil Street where they remain to this day. Eastgate Street was constructed from "The Lawn" or garden of Eastgate House and came into existence in 1850, initially being known as High Street Eastgate, but by 1851 the present name had been adopted. The first properties to be built in 1850, on the corner with The Broadway (Nos. 1,2 & 3), are now occupied by Bulthaup Kitchen Designs, B. Matthews Funeral Directors and Charles House Chinese Restaurant. Gradually the whole "new estate" was built including side streets such as Boundary Street, Lawn Street and Garden Lane. I am relating all these details as they have some bearing on the pubs and the brewery mentioned in chapter 3.

Close to the present Eastgate House was the *Mildmay Arms,* named after Dowager Lady Mildmay. The pub closed in the 1970s and the premises were converted into a veterinary practice called Mildmay Veterinary Centre who moved to Winnall in 2001. The property was given Listed Building status in March 2000 by the Department of Culture, Media & Sport, because of the *Mildmay Arms'* rare "silent clock". Prior to 1867 it was customary for patrons to obtain liquor on 'short credit', the record being chalked on a slate behind the bar. The County Court Act 1867, known as "The Slate Act", rendered the debts irrecoverable. The most favoured means of reminding customers of this was to place a 'silent clock' in a prominent position to denote that 'tick had ceased'. The landlord of the *Mildmay Arms* at that time placed the clock face on the gable of the pub as a courteous reminder to customers that 'tick' ceased at 11.50 p.m. on the day previous to the Act becoming operative. Developers wanted to knock down the historic building and initial proposals drew widespread opposition including

40. The *Mildmay Arms*, Eastgate Street. Closed in the 1970s. Now a private house No. 74 Eastgate Street. Note the "Silent clock" on the gable of the premises.　　　　*Photo: Author*

a petition with nearly 500 signatures. Eventually, the premises were saved and it is now a private house simply known as No. 74 Eastgate Street, tastefully restored by architect Huw Thomas, a council member of the Trust.

The *Poulterers' Rest* adjoined Tagart Morgan & Coles Ltd. Saw Mills in Lawn Street and lost its licence in 1940. The pub was demolished in the 1960s on the redevelopment of the Friarsgate area. Lawn House, a retirement home for the elderly, now stands on the site in the reconstructed Lawn Street.

The *Mash Tun,* whose rear beer-garden backs on to the River Itchen, was originally known as *The Lawn Tavern,* later changing its name to *The Fighting Cocks,* and now belongs to *Enterprise Inns.* Some years ago beer was brewed in the room at the rear of the premises. The pub underwent a complete refurbishment in October 2005 and reopened with a new pub sign showing a man stirring the mash tun with a stirring stick. A mash tun is a large vessel, complete with stirring implements, that would have held the mix of the cracked malt and hot water to produce wort.

The *Willow Tree Inn* is almost on an island fronting Durngate Place with its picturesque rear garden in a triangular shape divided by two streams. The pub originally belonged to *Winchester Brewery* and is now owned by *Greene King.* There is evidence of a fulling-mill, c.1500, possibly on the site of the pub as close by stood Durngate Mill, dating back to the reign of King John, which was demolished in 1966.

The *Waggon and Horses* stood on the corner of Union Street and Lower Brook Street, opposite the Fire Station. The pub, belonging to *Winchester Brewery,* was demolished in 1969 for the redevelopment of the Friarsgate area. Not far away at No. 56 Lower Brook Street stood Carhart's general stores where in 1963 the premises was the scene of a murder during the process of a robbery.

41. The *Mash Tun*, Eastgate Street. Originally known as *The Lawn Tavern* and then *The Fighting Cocks*. The launch "pad" for this book on 23 March 2007. *Photo: Author*

42. *Willow Tree Inn* is almost on an island fronting Durngate Place in a triangular shape divided by two streams. *Photo: Author*

Finally, in this section, the *Bird-in-Hand* stood on the opposite side of Union Street. The site is now occupied by the Moorside Nursing Home for the Frail.

SECTION II
Broadway to City Cross (Butter Cross)

Hastings-based architects Jeffery & Skiller were winners of an architectural competition for the design of the Gothic-styled Guildhall which was built between 1871 and 1873 by Joseph Bull *& Sons* of Southampton at the cost of £20,000. The foundation stone was laid by The Rt. Hon. Lord Viscount Eversley, High Steward, on 22 December 1871 and the building opened on 14 May 1873 by The Rt. Hon. Lord Selborne, the Lord High Chancellor of Great Britain. However before the commencement of building works, a pub had to be demolished and this was *The Globe,* a square three-storey house with a coal store, adjoining Abbey Passage, and a bowling green at the rear.

Obviously, the City Fathers decided within a short space of time that their new "home" was not large enough and so two years later in 1875 an extension was built on the site of the old Police Station at the cost of £2149. This stretches from Kings Court, adjoining the Tourist Information Centre, to the corner of Colebrook Street. Thomas Stopher Junr. was the architect for the extension which housed the School of Art in one section and in the other section the public library, which moved down in 1876 from the Old Guildhall, on the corner of High Street and St. Thomas Street, the site now occupied by Lloyds TSB. The words over the arches of the extension "School of Art" and "Public Reading Room" are still visible today. The Police Station moved over to the other side of the Guildhall, with the fire station next door, where the Saxon Suite is now situated. In 1892/3 the banqueting hall (now King Alfred Hall) was built, with further additions in 1894 including a pub known as the *Guildhall Tavern* which opened in 1895. Although the entrance is now from The Broadway, the postal address is still No. 57 Colebrook

43. *Guildhall Tavern,* opened in 1895, whose postal address is still No. 57 Colebrook Street although the main entrance is now from The Broadway.   *Photo: Author*

Street, where the original entrance used to be, with its frontal red-bricked and flint fascia. Over the front wall in tiled lettering are the words "Dorchester Ales & Stout – Eldridge Pope & Co. Ltd." When the library moved from the Guildhall to its present site in Jewry Street in October 1936, the pub was extended into the space vacated by the library – hence the entrance today from The Broadway. The venue is now operated by *Marston's PLC* as a Pitcher and Piano bar/restaurant. It is possible that a hotel by the name of *Albany* previously occupied this site. Incorporated into the main building, on the left-hand side, was a magistrates room, eventually converted into *The Abbey Bar*. Today it is known as *Wintonian's* named after citizens born and bred in Winchester.

There has been a pub on the site of the *Crown & Anchor* since the mid-19th century. The fascia sign printed at roof level of the front wall read "Winchester Brewery Co. Ltd." which means it is a *Greene King* pub today. The words further down on the wall read "Foreign Wines & Spirits". The original building was demolished to make way for the present pub, possibly in the late 1920s or early 1930s.

A bus station was required for the city and so the *New Town Hall Tavern*, formerly a *Winchester Brewery* pub, and the adjoining shops were demolished in 1934 to make way for Winchester's new Hants & Dorset Bus Station which opened on 20 June 1935 (one year later than the coach station in Worthy Lane). This accommodated Hants & Dorset and Aldershot & District buses only. The King Alfred buses still used the area

44. *Crown & Anchor*, The Broadway. The present building takes the place of the original alehouse on the site.   *Photo: Author*

by St. John's House for their passengers. The bus station is now owned by Stagecoach for their Hampshire buses, but at the time of this book's publication, there are plans to redevelop the whole of this area with a new bus station facing in the opposite direction emerging into Friarsgate. New shops were built on either side of the bus station and No. 164 is now an off-licence called *Wine Rack* owned by the *Thresher* chain.

The building next to Coral Betting Shop, empty at the time of publication, was *The Running Horse* with an archway separating it from the adjoining pub. The licence ceased in the early 1900s and the premises were converted into two shops in 1911/12. The property occupied by Coral Betting Shop was, at one time, an off-licence known as *Victoria Wines*.

The pub on the other side of the archway, formerly known as *India Arms* (not *Indian Arms* as mentioned in the pub story), was originally a coaching inn and the site of the stables can still be seen at the rear of the premises. The pub, appropriately called *The Old Coach House Inn*, was re-named *Alfie's* in February 2007. There is an original beam in one of the bars which gives the date "circa 1678 AD". In the days of "smoking-room" meetings, this inn was used a great deal by smaller tradesmen of the city but with the dying out of the "smoking-room" habit trade at the bar declined. A former *Watneys* pub, it now belongs to *Trust Inns Ltd.*

45. *The Old Coach House Inn*, The Broadway, originally known as *The India Arms*, and since February 2007, re-named *Alfie's*. *Photo: Author*

The High Street end of Colebrook Street was another "slum" area; all the houses and other buildings were demolished in the 1960s when this part of the city was redeveloped with a new hotel, council offices and a car-park.. At the far end of Colebrook Street stands a private dwelling (No. 101) opposite Colebrook Place. This was *The Masons' Arms*, referring, possibly, to stonemasons of the cathedral rather than the Winchester Lodge of Freemasons; there is no record that they ever met at the pub. One can still see the faded marking on the front wall which contained the name of the pub. The property ceased to be a licensed house in about 1924.

The *Royal Standard*, situated on land now occupied by *The Wessex Hotel*, was a *Colson* pub and, with surrounding dwellings, it became the victim of demolition in 1961/2. A lane ran alongside, appropriately called Amen Corner.

The *City Arms Inn,* now the Pizza Hut, was built in 1873/4 for Guy Pointer, who operated the *Chesil Brewery* (referred to in chapter 3), from the designs of Thomas Stopher Junr. at the cost of £1478. This took the place of the old *City Arms Inn,* which according to the notes of Thomas Stopher was a "rambling brick and tiled house with no distinctive feature....much frequented by local politicians and neighbouring tradesmen". The Winchester Lodge of Freemasons met at the pub from 1801 to 1806. The new *City Arms Inn* was purchased by the Misses Lousia and Emma Perks, at about the turn of the 20th century, for £6000. Previously, in 1898, the Misses Perks erected The Soldiers' Welcome Club on the corner of High Street and Colebrook Sreet, from the designs of Thomas Stopher Junr., at the cost of £350. This building is now known as The Welcome Gospel Hall.

The *City Arms Inn* closed in 1911 and the Misses Perks sold the premises to Winchester & District Co-operative Society "on condition that they gave up the license". Plans were approved for the conversion of the pub into shop premises and the words over the front fascia were "Grocery – Outfitters – Drapers". The Co-operative Society occupied the property for a number of years using the ground floor as their food hall with ladies fashions and menswear upstairs. Thomas Stopher remarked at the time of the transformation: "they spoilt my design by the shop fronts and majolica decorations" (ie: porous pottery glazed with bright metallic oxides).

The *Old Vine* in High Street stood on the site now occupied by Stead & Simpson Shoe Shop. The pub closed in 1912 on the refusal of the magistrates to renew its licence. The property was converted into a cheap hardware store known as The Peoples Bazaar which lasted until the building was demolished in 1925 with new shop premises erected the same year for Freeman Hardy & Willis Ltd. the predecessors of Stead & Simpson.

Although the postal address for *The Coach & Horses* was 145 High Street the pub stood at the rear of the site now occupied by Boots Opticians. The archway at the side of the present building, which is not original but a replica, led to the pub with the stables adjoining for the horses and carriages. The licensed premises closed in the early 1960s.

The *Suffolk Arms* and hotel stood on the corner of High Street and Middle Brook Street. The pub was demolished in 1934 to make way for the new Marks & Spencer store which opened in 1935. In the 13th century this area contained the old Cloth Hall. The former name of the pub was *Marquis of Granby,* named after a brilliant soldier much-loved by the men under his command. He lived from 1721 to 1770 and in 1760, during what has become known as the Seven Years War, he was in charge of cavalry with the army in Germany. Of his character it is said that he was "brave to a fault, skilful, generous to profuseness, careful of his men and beloved by them". After the wars, so the story goes, he set up many of his officers in taverns, thus making this pub's name a popular one throughout the country. The Marquis gave rise to a well-known phrase, as it was customary in his time to wear wigs even when in battle. But the bald-headed Marquis did not comply with this practice – hence the phrase "to go into something bald-headed". The Winchester Lodge of Freemasons held meetings there from 1816 to 1831. On the High Street wall of the pub were the words "John May & Co. Finest Ales & Stout".

46. The *Suffolk Arms* and hotel stood on the corner of High Street and Middle Brook Street. Demolished in 1934 to make way for the new Marks & Spencer store which opened the following year.   *Photo: Hampshire County Library*

Although, once again, the postal address for the *Old Bell & Crown* was 136 High Street, the pub laid back from High Street but later, shops were built in front of the premises, obstructing its view from the street. When this occurred the only way to obtain entrance to the licensed premises was through a narrow passageway from High Street. The pub stood on the foundations of an old church known as St. Mary Ode's. The notes of Thomas Stopher Junr. state: "it is now a favourite place for policemen, being well out of sight and with two exits". The pub ceased trading in 1922. The rear of the building, which fronted on to St. George's Street, was used as shop premises until demolition took place in 2003 to make way for the new Superdrug store. The original entrance is now engulfed in the extension of Marks & Spencer, on which stood The London Bazaar "local depot for Post Cards, Crest China and Souvenirs of the City" as well as being toy dealers. The proprietor was the father of Jo Gordon-Watson, another prominent member of the Trust.

To confuse matters further, on the opposite side of High Street stood the *New Bell & Crown*. The building was used as a pub by that name from 1867 to 1964 and belonged to *Strong & Co. of Romsey Ltd.* From 1964 to 1970 Martins Bank occupied the premises; they were taken over by Bradford & Bingley Building Society in 1970 who are still in possession of the building today.

Similar to the *Old Bell & Crown,* one can only obtain access to *The Bakers Arms* by going through a narrow passageway leading from High Street to Market Street known as Bakers Arms Passageway and, again the postal address is No. 22 High Street! A pub has been on this site since the 1750s; The Winchester Lodge of Freemasons, founded in 1761, held their first meetings in one of the oak-panelled rooms above the premises from that year to 1801. The old house, situated at the end of the present passage which was entirely closed in, proved very inconvenient. The owners, *Strong & Co. of Romsey Ltd.*, demolished the old building in 1897 and set about to widen the passageway, making access possible into Market Lane and at the same time rebuilt the pub. The present lessee, Michael Sinker, has been there for 34 years making him the city's longest-serving publican. The freehold now belongs to *Enterprise Inns*. *The Bakers Arms* always prides itself during summer months for the beautiful display of hanging baskets and other floral arrangements under the glass canopy, winning several awards over the years.

47. *The Bakers Arms*, off High Street. The present pub dates from c.1897.   *Photo: Author*

The Market Hall, on the corner of High Street and Market Street, dates from 1772. During 2004/5 the building underwent substantial alterations. Carphone Warehouse now occupy the unit once used by *Tyler & Co. Ltd.*, wine and spirit merchants. On the opposite side of High Street the premises now occupied by Nationwide Building Society was another off-licence trading under the name of *Peter Dominic Ltd.*

A wine store called *The City Wine Vaults* stood on the corner of High Street and Upper Brook Street, where Vodaphone trades today. The original building was demolished in 1933 and rebuilt for Dolcis Shoe Shop which came to Winchester in 1934.

There were three *White Horse* pubs in the city and one cannot fail to see where *The White Horse Inn* situated in High Street operated. The inn was rebuilt in flint and brick towards the end of the 19th century for Guy Pointer of the *Chesil Brewery* (referred to in chapter 3) but the pub finally lost its licence in 1936. The premises are built on the site of St. Mary Kalender Church. The family of Butts, the shoemakers, occupied the property for many years and the tradition in some ways continues with Clarks Shoe Shop now firmly in control. The Winchester Lodge of Freemasons held their meetings at the pub from 1831 to 1854.

48. *The White Horse Inn*, High Street, lost its licence in 1936. Clarks shoe shop now occupy the premises, but the sign is still clearly visible on the front wall.   *Photo: Author*

Finally, in this section, I am mentioning an inn which strictly should not be included as it closed in 1782 but many people go into these two shops without knowing that they are entering the site of a watering-hole in the 17th and 18th centuries. I refer to Caffè Nero and The Works bookshop opposite the City Cross, or Butter Cross, as some Wintonians call it. This fine building, with its bay windows, was *The Chequer's Inn* and wandering players performed in the yard during the Tudor period. There is some evidence that the area of the inn stretched as far as the premises on the corner of High Street and St. Peter Street.

SECTION III
City Cross to the West Gate

The Royal Oak stands along the passageway dividing High Street from St. George's Street known by the name of Royal Oak Passage. The pub is immediately opposite The House of God Begot (referred to in chapter 6). In fact, the eaves practically touch those of the restaurant, very similar to The Shambles in York. It is said to be "the oldest licensed bar in England". The lower Bar was first used to brew beer over 1000 years ago. Built as a public house in 1630 the premises were, by 1677, commonly known as *The Royal Oak*. The earliest reference to a pub on the site dates to 1390-1430. It gained the name *The Royal Oak* from the English Civil War. Once belonging to *Strong & Co. of Romsey Ltd.* it is now a *Greene King* pub. In the 18th century a John Bull was landlord of the inn which is literally in the butchers' shambles, the name coming from the "shamnels" meaning the stalls or benches on which meat was displayed; St. Peter Street, at one time, was known as Fleshmonger Street, the Norman name for Butchers Street. This was the boundary of the Jewish ghetto until 1290 when they were expelled from the kingdom during the reign of Edward I as they were engaged in the business of money lending which was forbidden to Christians.

49. *The Royal Oak*, off High Street. The pub dates from 1630.   *Photo: Author*

On the opposite side of High Street by the corner of St. Thomas Street is a shop called Elvi Fashions but the building was originally *Ye Dolphin Inn*. This was the third pub on the site, there having been licensed premises here for centuries. The old *Dolphin Inn*, a quaint two-storey building in half-timbered work, was replaced in 1882 by Richard Moss (see chapter 4) to the designs of Thomas Stopher Junr. with a new purpose-built pub of Elizabethan-style in the ownership of *Winchester Brewery*. The building was erected over cellars of a medieval tavern which stood on the site. The existing pub closed in 1981 when a £500,000 facelift turned the premises into shops and offices. The words *Ye Dolphin Inn* are impressed in the stonework over the front door of the fashion shop. Keen eyes will spot the dolphin figures on either side of the doorway. These are replicas of the original ones. The property now belongs to St. John's Hospital & Allied Charities. Included in the same block is an off-licence called *Nicolas*.

50. *Ye Dolphin Inn* on the corner of High Street and St. Thomas Street. The present building dates from 1882. The pub closed in 1981 and the premises is now a shop known as Elvi Fashions. *Photo: Author*

Further up High Street and opposite Southgate Street stands a building once used by Southampton & District Gas Undertaking for their offices and showrooms (No.90) and Westminster Bank Ltd. (No.91) before the latter was merged with National Provincial Bank Ltd. to become NatWest based at 105 High Street. Both properties were converted into a modern pub called *The Fugue & Firkin*, later renamed *O'Neills Irish Bar*. *O'Neills* belongs to *Mitchells & Butlers* chain of pubs.

Your Move, estate agents, is situated on the corner of High Street and Staple Gardens, which was at one time, called Star Lane. On this site stood *The Star Inn* which was demolished in 1885 and rebuilt to the design of Thomas Stopher Junr. for Guy Pointer of the *Chesil Brewery* (referred to in chapter 3) at the cost of £2448. Thomas Stopher stated in his notes: "three skeletons were found in digging for the foundations of the new building, all buried in an upright squatting position in square cists plastered with clay. They were evidently very early burials". The name changed to *The Talbot Hotel* in 1929. Unfortunately, the estate agents' board hides the words "Strong & Co. of Romsey Ltd." which are imprinted on the front wall over the windows that display properties for sale.

One of the most famous pubs in Winchester was *The Plume of Feathers,* previously known as *The Fighting Cocks.* This pub adjoined the West Gate and had two entrances; one on the Tower Street side and the other from the opposite side of the West Gate. In the 1820s the licensed premises was described as a "homely domestic building". It was remodelled in the 19th century by Thomas Stopher Junr. with inappropriate castellated false fronts on either side complete with a mock tower. This was on the Upper High Street side of the building. The room over the West Gate was an annexe to the pub before being converted into a museum in 1898. This was used as a smoking-room, known in old documents as the "Porter's Lodge" of the West Gate. Smoking-rooms were, according to an article in the *Hampshire Chronicle* on *Old Winchester Inns* dated 31 March 1888, "the centre of conversational communication and enjoyment after the apron was hung up and the eight o'clock suppers eaten". There were two signs on the front wall of the Tower Street side; on the top "The Plume of Feathers" and lower down the words "Strong & Co. of Romsey Ltd" but on the mock tower the board read "Plume of Feathers – Wootten & Co's entire" (sic) which indicates that Strong's took over the *Lion Brewery* referred to in chapter 3.

51. *The Plume of Feathers,* from High Street side of West Gate. The pub, previously known as *The Fighting Cocks,* was demolished in 1938.   *Photo: Hampshire County Library*

The pub was demolished in 1938 to make way for the new County Council offices and the road around the 13th century West Gate. World War II, however, intervened and the building programme was delayed until the 1950s when the road alongside the old city gate opened in 1956 followed by the new County Council offices which HM the Queen opened in June1959 – hence the name Queen Elizabeth II Court.

On the opposite side, adjacent to the West Gate, is a red-bricked building used today as offices by Hampshire County Council. This was the *Westgate Hotel & Tavern* from August 1861. After the County Council Act 1888 came into force, the flint-built offices erected on Castle Hill from 1892 to 1894 were one of the first county council offices to be built in the country and, at the same time, the hotel and tavern was taken over by the County Council. Prior to the flint buildings shops occupied the site. My grandfather, James Yates, a wig-maker and gents hairdresser, occupied one of the shops. I possess a faded photograph taken c.1871 with him standing outside his barber's shop.

52. *Westgate Hotel & Tavern*, Castle Hill adjoining the West Gate existed from 1861 to c.1893. Today the building is used as offices for Hampshire County Council.   *Photo: Author*

After the closure of the *Westgate Hotel & Tavern,* the building on the corner of Upper High Street and Romsey Road (formerly a chemists and druggists) became *Westgate Hotel* in 1894. The deeds show that Mr. Eldridge and Mr. Pope purchased the property in 1893 and converted it into a pub/hotel. On the front wall were the words "Eldridge Pope" and "Westgate Hotel". *Eldridge Pope* operated the pub from 1894 to 2004.

Although based in Dorset, perhaps mention should be made of this famous brewery and the pubs in the city associated with the company. Founded in 1837, the brewery was built at Dorchester in 1874 and the logo on all its pub signs was that of "the huntsman". In October 2004 the brewery closed, which at the time of publication is the subject of a plan to build up to 550 homes on the site. The 151-strong chain of *Eldridge Pope* pubs, mainly situated in the south and south-west of the country, was sold for £42.3million in October 2004 to entrepreneur Michael Cannon who has been involved in the industry for over 30 years. However, on 8 January 2007 *Wolverhampton & Dudley Breweries* changed its name to *Marston's PLC* and on 25 January 2007 the brewery acquired all of *Eldridge Pope's* pubs which now come under the banner of *Marston's PLC.*

The name changed from *Westgate Hotel* to *The Westgate Inn* in 2005 to comply with EU regulations. To be called a hotel, apparently, proprietors of inns are obliged to have 24-hour reception, a lift and other facilities which *The Westgate Inn* does not possess, although it was completely refurbished in 2005. The wording at roof level of the building still bears the name of *Westgate Hotel,* so do the frontal windows of the premises. It is now a *Marston's PLC* pub/hotel.

53. *The Westgate Inn*, on the corner of Upper High Street and Romsey Road. Originally a private house, it was converted into the *Westgate Hotel* in 1894. Renamed *The Westgate Inn* in 2005.   *Photo: Author*

SECTION IV
The Brooks and Silver Hill

There were 18 public houses in the three streets known as The Brooks – now only a night-club remains. In addition, at least four beer-houses operated in this area.

The definition of a brook is "a natural freshwater river"; this part of Winchester is surrounded by water both below and at ground level. Excavations over recent years have shown that in the pre-Roman period a flood plain extended between Parchment Street and Union Street which would have included The Brooks. The Romans diverted the River Itchen into an artificial channel and the present course of the river, by the Weirs, still follows the route set by the Roman engineers. King Alfred constructed three tributaries from the Itchen which flow through the recreation ground and public park at North Walls and at least one of them continues its direction under Park Avenue and Middle Brook Street. This is the main reason why the lower part of the city is subjected to flooding as evidenced by the great flood of 2000, severely damaging St. Bede's School which backs on to the park land.

The Brooks was another poor working-class area of the city until major re-development took place in the late 1950s and early 1960s when the remains of several medieval houses were discovered including that of John de Tytyng, a Tudor merchant.

Because of these extensive development plans it meant that I have had difficulty in locating the exact position of all the pubs in this section. Where some are shown on the 1870 Ordnance Survey map I have been able to "pin-point" them or, alternatively, identify others from the old *Warren's* or *Kelly's* street directories.

We start with Lower Brook Street and the first pub I came across on the map was *The Butchers' Arms* which stood on the site now occupied by the Tanner Street multi-storey car-park. This pub closed in 1912. *The Catherine Wheel* is identified on the same map as standing on the right-hand corner of Friarsgate and Lower Brook Street which is now occupied by Godson House residential flats for the elderly. The pub lost its licence in the 1940s. Jewells Iron Factory stood opposite and workers visited the pub for a lunchtime drink! Cossack Lane House is built on the site of the depository that belonged to White & Co. Ltd. On the right-hand side of this building (towards High Street) were two pubs, the *Britannia Arms,* closed in 1912, and *Red White & Blue,* which ceased trading in 1908. *The White Hart* stood on the left-hand side of the depository (going towards North Walls). A *Colson* pub, it closed in 1923. There were two pubs in Winchester by the name of *The Rose & Crown,* the first being in this street; it stood on the site at present occupied by Marks & Spencer's car-park and loading bay, close to St. Clement's Surgery. The pub closed in the year that the First World War started, 1914.

Moving to Middle Brook Street, the first watering-hole from High Street was *The Duke of Wellington,* named after "The Iron Duke" who routed Napoleon at Waterloo in 1815 and later became Prime Minister (1828-30). This stood on the Marks & Spencer corner with St. George's Street. The pub closed in 1907.

I believe *The Old House at Home* stood near the site now occupied by Waterstones, booksellers. This pub belonged to *Lion Brewery,* referred to in chapter 3, and closed in 1904. A short distance away, on the corner of The Brooks Shopping Centre and Friarsgate, stood *The Bricklayer's Arms* which ceased trading in 1915. *The Winton Ale House* was situated at the far end of Lansdowne Terrace next to Friary House, HQ Hampshire Probation Board. The pub closed in 1928/9. *The Beehive,* which ceased trading in 1906, stood on the site now occupied by Winchester Parking Office. The *Robin Hood* is identified on the map as standing on the corner of Middle Brook Street with Cossack Lane, which still survives, although the few houses that made up the lane with Trinity School and Bull Bros. contractors' yard, have long since disappeared. The pub lost its licence in 1941. Friary House occupies the site today.

The last pub in the city to sell only beer was *The John Barleycorn* which stood on part of the car-park, now used regularly for the Sunday Farmers' Market, opposite Winchester Family Church, formerly the Ritz Cinema. Filmgoers would cross over the street from the cinema for a drink, after enjoying three hours of "family entertainment", before returning to their homes – there were no bars at cinemas in those days! The licensed premises, a *Colson* pub, was demolished in 1964 to make way for the car-park and the buildings close by including the General Post Office which moved to its position from Parchment Street in 1966. The *Victoria Inn,* built in 1881 of mock-Tudor design, stood on the corner of Middle Brook Street and Silver Hill, where the entrance to King's Walk shopping arcade is today. The pub was demolished in 1971.

54. *Victoria Inn,* on corner of Middle Brook Street and Silver Hill. Built in 1881 and demolished in 1971.   *Photo: Hampshire County Library*

Silver Hill covers a very short distance between Middle Brook Street and Lower Brook Street but, somehow, two inns were crammed into that space – plus a Methodist Chapel!

In fact, the postal address of the *Victoria Inn* was Nos. 1 & 2 Silver Hill after which came the *Coachmaker's Arms,* dating from c. 1860 and at the end of "the hill" stood the *Skinner's Arms;* both pubs closed in 1907. In between them, the first Methodist Chapel in Winchester was positioned, dedicated on 24 November 1785 by Revd John Wesley, the founder of Methodism, aged 82 at the time. A Sunday School was established there in 1876 but the chapel faltered by 1900. Several uses were made of the buildings over the years including workshops for Dicks Ltd. heating, electrical and refrigeration engineers (whose retail shop in High Street was next to Freeman Hardy & Willis Ltd.) and R.M. Stanbrook, tool merchant, ironmonger and hardware stores. Harold Phillis, the watch and clockmaker, who maintained the Town Clock above Lloyds TSB, also worked from there. The buildings were demolished in 1971 to make way for the King's Walk shopping arcade.

The name Silver Hill, which is not a hill at all, possibly has its origin from the name of a trade; there was a goldsmith working in Silver Hill in the early 13th century.

Upper Brook Street boasted four pubs, a beer-house, a tap and a brewery – the only remaining venue of this kind in The Brooks is along the street and that's a night-club! The building on the corner with St. George's Street, now the offices of the *Hampshire Chronicle*, *NewsExtra* and *Daily Echo*, dates from the early 18th century. This was a pub known as *The Plough* which closed in 1954. When repairs were made to the building in 1959 the carved stones now embedded in the St. George's Street side wall were found in excavations. One stone is Saxon work of the 9th century and the others are Norman. Some bricks from a Roman building are also built into the wall. The stonework possibly came from the church of St. Ruel, the site of which lies to the south of the premises now known as No. 5 Upper Brook Street.

55. *The Plough*, on the corner of St. George's Street and Upper Brook Street, dating from the early 18th century, closed in 1954. Now the Offices of *Hampshire Chronicle*, *NewsExtra* and *Daily Echo*.   *Photo: Author*

The *Nightingale Inn* stood on the site of the night-club, formerly a pub called *The Original Porthouse* but following a £1.2million refurbishment the venue, now part of Tattershall Castle Group (TCG Aquisitions Ltd.), reopened on 14 October 2006 with the name changed to *Porthouse Bar & Nightclub*. The present building was erected in the 1970s as a pub known as *The Fountainhead* operated by *Eldridge Pope*. The *Nightingale Inn* was named after Florence Nightingale, the British nurse (1820-1910), known as *The Lady with the Lamp*, noted for her work during the Crimean War. As a Hampshire resident she was in favour of moving the hospital from Parchment Street, where No. 64 is today, to the present position at the top of Romsey Road, because of the deterioration of the building, its cramped situation in central Winchester and "the unwillingness of the corporation to provide mains drainage".

56. *The Original Porthouse*, Upper Brook Street, originally *The Fountainhead* public house. Now a night-club known since October 2006 as *Porthouse Bar & Nightclub*. Photo taken August 2006 before the refurbishment took place.　　　　　　　　*Photo: Author*

The *Queen's Head*, referred to in "About The Trust" chapter, stood on the site now occupied by the Upper Brook Street entrance to The Brooks Shopping Centre. In the late 18th-century the pub was the headquarters of the Winchester/London carriers. At one time it belonged to *Strong & Co. of Romsey Ltd.* After demolition of the pub and other properties in the late 1950s the whole area became a car-park before the erection of the present shopping centre. Another pub by the name of *New Queen's Head* emerged in Stanmore Lane (see Section X of this chapter for details).

57. *The Queen's Head*, Upper Brook Street which the Trust endeavoured to save. Demolished late 1950s.　　　　　　　*Photo: Winchester Museums, Winchester City Council*

There were two *Gardener's Arms* in Winchester; the first stood partly on the site of the Telephone Exchange built in 1942 by Taylor Woodrow Ltd. The pub closed in 1935.

A beer-house has existed at No. 47 Upper Brook Street since 1887 and belonged to *Chesil Brewery*. Keith Bros. ran the wine shop from 1932 until 1987, the whole block being modernized in the 1980s. It is now a *Thresher* Wine Shop. The site has been associated with alcoholic drink for 120 years.

SECTION V
North Walls and Parchment Street

Opposite Upper Brook Street in North Walls stood two pubs virtually next door to one another. The *Rose and Shamrock* (No. 18) closed in 1916 and *The Three Tuns* (No. 23) closed early in the 1960s when it became the Winchester Excavations Hostel until the whole area was demolished in the late 1960s. The gap now forms the pedestrian entrance to St. Peter's car-park

On the corner of North Walls and Parchment Street *The North Walls* (formerly known as *The Foresters' Arms* and *The Forester)* has been there since before 1873. It belongs to the *Greene King* chain and after extensive refurbishment the venue reopened in March 2007 as a bar/restaurant.

58. *The North Walls*, formerly known as *The Foresters' Arms* and *The Forester*. Photo taken August 2006 before the refurbishment took place and name changed.   *Photo: Author*

The *Fountain Inn,* now Scope charity shop, was for many years *Eldridge Pope's* wine shop which closed in 1966. Another wine shop existed on the opposite side of the street at No. 9a run by *Godrich & Petman*. Later the premises became an arts centre called The North Pole before its recent conversion into Boudoir Blush, a lingerie and swimwear boutique. *Godrich & Petman* had another wine shop on the corner of High Street and The Square, now West Cornwall Pasty Co. The company also operated *The Carpenter's Arms* referred to in section VIII of this chapter.

The *Post Office Tavern* was swallowed up by the widening of St. George's Street in the late 1950s. It stood on the corner of Parchment Street and St. George's Street and was a *Winchester Brewery* pub. My father's gents hairdressing salon adjoined the premises, now rebuilt as J. Collin & Son, Jewellers.

The *Royal Tap,* connected to the *Royal Hotel* in St. Peter Street, possibly stood at the rear where the hotel's car-park is today.

Finally, in this section, I am including the building on the corner of Parchment Street and St. George's Street which is now occupied by Ladbrokes and The Forte Tearooms. This was *The Red Lion* from 1664, in the days of Charles II, which continued into the 19th century. How do I know this? Jeffrey Smith, a vice-president and a founder member of the Trust, produced the original deed of the premises which he owns. For many years Jeffrey's firm of auctioneers, chartered surveyors and estate agents, trading under the name of George Smith & Son, operated from there.

SECTION VI
Market Street, The Square, Kingsgate Street and Kingsgate Road

It is clear to see the date when the *Old Market Inn* on the corner of Market Street and The Square was built. In large figures high on the front wall is "c.1860". The pub is so named because there was a street market dating from the 14th century in the area. At the commencement of the street stood Thomasesgate which was the main entrance to the cathedral precinct. The land inside the gate formed part of the cathedral's burial ground. The pub belonged to *Whitbreads* at one time but it is now part of the *Enterprise Inns* group.

The *Napoleon* stood opposite the *Old Market Inn* and the premises, 3a The Square, is today used as offices. The pub closed in 1901. The *Nelson Arms,* obviously named after Lord Nelson, is now Dinghams cook and fireplaces shop. The pub dated back to c.1812.

The building forming the rear entrance to Boots, the chemists, was *The Lamb* which existed from 1762 to 1870.

The *Eclipse Inn* dates back to 1580 and is built on the graveyard of the cathedral. Originally the rectory of the church of St. Lawrence-in-the-Square, it became an alehouse c.1750 and then a pub in the 1800s. The name "Eclipse" comes from the story that the alehouse became more popular than the nearby *Sun Inn* (No.10) and thereby eclipsed it! The plaster covering the timber-framing was removed in the 1920s when the building was restored.

59. *Old Market Inn*, on the corner of Market Street and The Square, dating from c.1860.

Photo: Author

We now come to the first ghost story in the book! The ghost of Lady Alicia Lisle (sometimes called Dame Alicia Lisle), a supporter of Cromwell, resided at Moyles Court near Ellingham, a village north of Ringwood. At the age of seventy, sheltering three fugitives of Monmouth's defeated army, she was arrested and tried by the dreaded Judge Jeffreys at the Assize and Quarter Sessions, known as "Bloody Assizes", in the Great Hall of the former Winchester Castle, in 1685. He sentenced her to be "burnt at the stake" but with public outcry and petition the sentence was commuted to

60. *The Eclipse Inn*, The Square, dates back to 1580. Originally the rectory of the church of St. Lawrence-in-the-Square, it became an alehouse c.1750.

Photo: Author

beheading. Alicia Lisle spent her last days in a small room on the top floor of the inn before execution on a scaffold outside *The Eclipse.* Her spirit returns from time to time haunting her little room and passageway on the upper floor of the pub. The landlord told me his cat refuses to go anywhere near that room! The pub also belongs to the *Enterprise Inns* group.

The Sun, facing *The Eclipse,* is built on the site of a church and The Hambledon shop now occupies the building.

Originally an inn dating from the 18th century with medieval cellars and Saxon foundations, a section of *The Old Vine,* which is strictly in Great Minster Street, became *Courage & Co*'s wine shop from 1884 amalgamating with the rest of the pub again in 1964. It also belongs to the *Enterprise Inns* group. In April 2005 the inn became Winchester's first "smoke-free" pub on its reopening after complete refurbishment.

Not one but two ghosts are said to haunt the premises, the first being Emily, a maid who was killed, or murdered, in the cellar in the 19th century. She is heard weeping on the stairs of the cellar from time to time. The second ghost is believed to be of a gentleman in a top floor room (again!) who turns switches on and lights up cigars in an ashtray!

The pub has stunning views across the cathedral and is only a short distance from High Street. The brochure states that "Italian, Spanish, French and Portuguese are spoken here".

61. *The Old Vine*, Great Minster Street, dates from the 18th century. It became Winchester's first "smoke-free" pub in April 2005.   *Photo: Author*

The Slug and Lettuce is another "modern" fashionable "drinking-hole". Originally two shops, a toy one known as The Pooh Shop and Holland & Barrett, health stores, the premises were tastefully converted into a pub in 1998. and won a "Design Award" presented by the Trust in 2000. It belongs to the *Laurel Pub Company.*

Walking through The Close and under the 12th-century Kingsgate Arch we come to one of the most famous pubs in Winchester, *The Wykeham Arms* situated on the corner of Kingsgate Street and Canon Street, neatly sandwiched between the College and the Cathedral. An 18th-century inn, built in 1755, it was originally known as *Fleur-de-Lys,* being the former royal arms of France, but the name changed c.1834 after the Napoleonic Wars to *The Wykeham Arms.* William of Wykeham was not only the Bishop of Winchester (1366-1404) but also the founder of Winchester College and New College, Oxford and Lord Chancellor of England. Anthony Trollope (1815-1882), the novelist, who wrote his first Barchester novel *The Warden* in 1855, was educated at Winchester College and The Hospital of St. Cross gave him the idea for his Barchester Chronicles, although the chief inspiration was Salisbury. On staying at *The Wykeham Arms* he described the pub as "a very ancient and third rate hostelry which my father preferred, partly because he thought the charges might be less there, but mainly because it is situated in the vicinity of the College and he had known and used it of old". The pub, however, is very different today winning several awards over recent years, mainly due to the late Graham Jameson who was its popular landlord. The awards included: Good Hotel Guide – "Cesar Ritz Award", Egon Ronay – "Pub of the Year for the United Kingdom", Good Pub Guide – "Wine Pub of the Year", "Pub Caterer of the Year", Which Hotel Guide – "the most preferred hotel in the South and South East of England" and in 2003 it was named Les Routiers "Wine Pub of the Year for the south and south East of England".

62. *The Wykeham Arms*, on the corner of Canon Street and Kingsgate Street. Built in 1755 it was originally known as *Fleur-de-Ly*s; name changed c.1834.   *Photo: Author*

For several years the pub belonged to *Gales Brewery* of Horndean, but as mentioned in chapter 5, the company was purchased in November 2005 by *Fuller's* of *The Griffin Brewery* Chiswick West London and so *The Wykeham Arms* is now part of their chain of pubs.

The present managers, Peter and Kate Miller, continue with the tradition of high standards set by Graham Jameson, for in November 2006, the famous watering-hole was named by *Fuller's* as "their Town and Local Pub of the Year".

The Wykeham Arms has associations with Lord Nelson who is reputed to have visited his mistress, Lady Hamilton, where she had accommodation. This is the reason why, on entering the venue, the customer encounters *The Nelson Bar* before passing through to *The Hamilton Bar*. On the 200th anniversary of the Battle of Trafalgar on 21 October 2005 there were celebrations in the bars and a special beer was brewed called "Trafalgar 200, 10 per cent Ale".

Incorporated in the premises are *The Bishop Bar* (after Wykeham) and *The Jameson Room* in memory of Graham Jameson. *The Wykeham Arms* celebrated its 250th anniversary on 24 September 2005 with a Fair in The Close opened by the then Dean of Winchester, The Very Revd Richard Till. The Cathedral Choir provided the music and George Gale Brands, the previous owners of the pub, created a special 250th anniversary beer. Their famous shire-horses and beer trailer were present and Peter Miller dressed up as William of Wykeham. The Dean said: "It is a very special watering-hole – long may it flourish". It is also a "dog-friendly" pub. There is no connection, by the way, between Emma Hamilton and Hamilton House which stands on the corner of Canon Street and Culver Road. This is named after the Duke of Hamilton (1606-49), Scottish adviser to Charles I but it was eventually used by Josephine Butler as "a refuge for fallen women" before she donated the property to the Salvation Army in 1887.

Continuing into Kingsgate Road we come to the *Queen Inn* which has been in existence since before 1860 and now belongs to *Greene King*. The pub sign is unusual as it depicts the "Queen of Hearts" from a deck of cards.

63. *Queen Inn*, Kingsgate Road. Note the pub sign which depicts the Queen of Hearts from a deck of cards.
Photo: Author

SECTION VII
St. Cross

Today we call this district of Winchester by the familiar name of St. Cross mainly because of its association with the almshouses but the area was originally known as the village of Sparkford. Its chapel, in the parish of St. Faith, was dedicated to the Holy Cross. The word "ford" means "a river crossing" and there was a Saxon monastery in the vicinity with a ford; therefore we have Sparkford Road, off St. James' Lane, where the University of Winchester (formerly King Alfred's College) is situated. There is also Sparkford House in St. Cross Road which had four pubs – now only one remains and that is *The Bell Inn,* believed, at one time, to be two houses but the building has been a pub since before 1860 and stands at the entrance to the Hospital of St. Cross, referred to in chapter 3.

Four doors from *The Bell Inn* stands a house with an interesting history which was the other *Gardener's Arms.* The land originally belonged to Winchester College and the property was built as two houses in 1675. It became one house in the 1700s with an extension made in 1847 when it became a pub. The first publican, Mr. Whale, was also a gardener – hence the name *Gardener's Arms* which ceased to be a pub in 1914 when it reverted to a private house and sold by Winchester College in the early 1920s. It was a *Woottons* pub.

64. *The Bell Inn* stands at the entrance to the Hospital of St. Cross.   *Photo: Author*

Going along St. Cross Road towards Winchester there were two pubs which faced one another. On the corner with Cripstead Lane stood *The White Horse,* (the second one) trading since before 1880, which is now a private residence. The marking on the front wall where the name of the pub used to be is still visible. The pub sign hangs over the front door with a delightful painting, within its frame, of children striding through a farm gate looking at cattle in a field, with St. Catherine's Hill in the background. The pub closed c.1990. On the opposite side of the road was *The Wheatsheaf*, again now converted into a private house. This pub, designed by Thomas Stopher Junr. c.1880, was operated by *Eldridge Pope* who transferred it into a high class wine shop in the late 1970s, finally closing c.1990. The sign, with the empty frame, still hangs over the front door. On the side wall of the property are the words "Ale & Stout drawn from the wood".

SECTION VIII
Southgate Street, St. Clement Street, St. Thomas Street and Little Minster Street

The Green Man stands on the corner of Southgate Street with St. Swithun Street. There has been a pub on this site from the early 1800s, originally known as *Green Man Inn*. On the front wall were painted the words "Wines & Spirits Genuine as Imported Wholesale and Retail". *The Green Man* was rebuilt and enlarged in 1881 for Richard Moss from designs by Thomas Stopher Junr. at the cost of £1395 to become a smart tavern, three storeys high, to replace the homely old wayside inn. Rebuilt in pseudo-Gothic style with flint and brick and terracotta ornaments on elaborate dormers it is a prominent feature of this part of the city. The name *The Green Man* has been worked in stone below the top corner window. The skittles alley at the rear of the pub was originally stables. Formerly a *Winchester Brewery* pub, it now belongs to *Greene King*. Excavations opposite the pub in 1971 revealed the Roman south gate to the city, the replacement of which was demolished in 1771.

There has been a pub on the corner of Southgate Street and St. Clement Street for over 200 years called *The Exchange* which derives its title from the 18th century when the pub was the first building in the city to carry a fire mark, that of The Exchange Fire Assurance Co. In 1887 Charles Sherry, the manager of the *Black Swan Hotel*, took over the licence. The first window on the St Clement Street side of the pub contains the words "Foreign wines" and "Ales & Stout". The venue now belongs to the *Enterprise Inns* group.

On the opposite corner estate agents by the name of Halifax Estate Agency occupy No.9 which, at one time, was *The Waterloo*, presumably named after the famous battle of 1815. The pub closed in 1890. For many years these premises were used by Collis Cobb & Harrison's Dairies Ltd.

There was just one pub in St. Clement Street called *Hampshire House* (No. 10) which belonged to Colson's *Chesil Brewery*. It closed in 1931 and the following year Tylers Chocolate Manufacturers used the property for storage. Mr. Tyler, a manufacturer and retailer of specialised chocolates, produced them for sale at his shop in Jewry Street (now Café de Paris) until the 1970s. His business was taken over by Bendicks of Mayfair (referred to in chapter 3). No. 10 then became part of the *Hampshire Chronicle* which they used as their photographer's department and training rooms until October 2004. The property was sold in September 2006 to Peagreen who design textiles and ceramics for retailers including Habitat and Paperchase.

65. *The Exchange*, on the corner of St. Clement Street and Southgate Street. There has been a pub on this site for over 200 years.   *Photo: Author*

66. *Hampshire House*, St. Clement Street. Pub closed in 1931. Then used by chocolate manufacturers followed by the *Hampshire Chronicle*.   *Photo: Hampshire Chronicle*

On the corner of St. Clement Street and St. Thomas Street is a ladies hairdressers salon called Blinkers. This was originally *The Brewery Tap* which, again, closed in 1931. Simpkins & Titler Ltd. furnisher dealers, upholsterers, cabinet makers and house decorators, then used the premises for their workshop. Further along St. Thomas Street (No. 20) stood *The Carpenter's Arms* run by *Godrich & Petman* of Parchment Street. This venue closed in 1907 and the property now forms part of Mason's Yard, named after Mr. H. Mason, the builder, who occupied this area for his workshop and yard which has now been converted into private dwellings.

67. *The Brewery Tap*, on the corner of St. Clement Street and St. Thomas Street, closed in
    1931. Now a ladies hairdressing salon called Blinkers.   *Photo: Author*

A pub called *King's Head Inn* stood at No. 17 Little Minster Street and dated from c.1660 or earlier. It had a charming old front with two gables and a picturesque yard at the rear – hence today we have the Kings Head Yard which connects Little Minster Street with St. Thomas Street. The pub closed in 1934 and was demolished in 1936. Painted on the front wall were the words "King's Head Inn – Wines & Spirits" and a notice by the entrance read "Stout & Ales". Next door, on the left-hand side, stood *Sadlers Brewery* (see chapter 3). On the right-hand side was Minster Garage. The site of the pub is now occupied by Blooms, specialising in Dutch flowers and chocolates.

The Winchester Lodge of Freemasons met there from 1806 to 1816. Jonathan Inggs, a 24-year-old waiter at *The George* and *White Hart* Hotels was appointed Tyler of the Lodge in 1805 and took up his duties the following year. A tyler is the officer who prepares the room in advance and guards the door during meetings. Jonathan resigned from that position early in 1819 due to ill-health but then became the inn's publican. However, this was short-lived and he died on 24 October 1819 at the early age of 38. He is buried in The Close not far from the west door of the Cathedral. His headstone was restored in November 2005 after vandals destroyed the original one in the early 1970s.

68. *King's Head Inn*, Little Minster Street. Dated from c.1660; closed 1934 and demolished 1936.
Photo: Hampshire County Library

SECTION IX
Canon Street

The residents of Canon Street were well served with public houses for their nightly "tipple", having five. After all, this was the "red light" district of Winchester and a "slum" area into the bargain! As mentioned in "About the Trust" the houses in this street nearly fell victim to demolition and redevelopment of the area, similar to Wales Street. In fact, dwellings at the top of the street were pulled down and council houses built – but the street was saved, mainly due to the involvement of the newly-formed Winchester Preservation Trust, and today in the words of estate agents, "It is a very desirable area of Winchester".

As Alderman Mrs G. Crompton (first woman Mayor of Winchester in 1946) commented in January 1956 that "given a few years, Canon Street would become one of the prettiest little streets in Winchester, inhabited by people who want to live in small economic houses of character in the centre of the city".

So, let us start from the Kingsgate Street end and work our way up the hill of this quaint street. *The Sportsman's Arms* which stood on the right-hand side closed in 1911 and the premises were demolished some years ago. A new development is now on the site. *The Albert,* next door to *The Sportsman's Arms,* closed in 1903 and is now a private residence known as The Malt House. The *Rose & Crown* (No. 47), just below St. Swithun's Villas, ceased trading in 1905 and again today is a private dwelling. Near to the old St. Michael's Church Hall, converted into a residential property, stood the third *White Horse*. This pub was the last watering-hole in Canon Street and lasted until c.1974 when the premises were demolished. New houses (Nos. 29, 29a and 30) now occupy the site. Finally, near to the top of the street, on the left-hand side, stood *The Perseverance* (No. 87), closing in 1956, before being converted into a private dwelling.

SECTION X
Romsey Road and Stanmore

The part of Romsey Road from the West Gate to Clifton Road (above the railway bridge) was, at one time, called St. James Street and the first pub we come to is *The St. James Tavern* which stands on the corner of Romsey Road and Crowder Terrace. It dates from at least 1860 and is a listed building. Framed on the wall of the pub is an Indenture dated 1867 and this venue is mentioned in the schedule of the deed. It now belongs to *Wadworth* of Devizes.

69. *The St. James Tavern*, on the corner of Romsey Road and Crowder Terrace, is a listed building dating from at least 1860.   *Photo: Author*

Although based in Wiltshire, I should mention this famous brewery and the two pubs in the city associated with the company, the other being *The Golden Lion* referred to in section I of this chapter. Founded in 1875 Wadworth's *Northgate Brewery*, with its impressive Victorian façade, was designed and built by Henry Wadworth in 1875 and is still run as a family business by his descendants.

The Hero stood on the right-hand side of the road, almost opposite *The St. James Tavern*. It ceased trading in 1906 and became a private dwelling-house the following year. The row of houses (Nos. 22 to 34 Romsey Road) were demolished in 1974 and apartments now occupy the site known as Arbour Court. The pub had been in existence since before 1860. Along the entire frontage was a chain-link "hitching-post" where horses were tethered to rings attached to the post, a small section of which still remains to this day. The County Museum took steps to prevent its destruction on demolition of the pub building just in case the "hitching-post" had some folk-history value.

If you have ever been unfortunate enough to attend or be admitted to the Accident and Emergency Department of The Royal Hampshire County Hospital, you may like to know that a pub stood on this site known as *The Battery Inn.* It was designed by Thomas Stopher Junr. and built in 1854. This was traditionally the pub for prison officers and hospital staff. The pub was demolished in the late 1970s to make way for the A & E Department.

The *County Arms,* on the corner of Romsey Road and Queen's Road, was built in 1848 with extensions made over the years. Refurbished in 2005, it is now a *Greene King* pub and at the time of publication the licensees were planning to display photographs of stars who had appeared at the Theatre Royal in recent years. Students from the West Downs Campus of the University of Winchester on the opposite side of Romsey Road are regular customers of the pub!

70. *The County Arms,* on the corner of Romsey Road and Queen's Road, built in 1848. Several extensions have been made to the pub over the years.   *Photo: Author*

Plans were passed for the erection of a hotel and pub by *Eldridge Pope* at the top of Stanmore Lane in 1929 and the *Stanmore Hotel* was eventually opened in 1933. An extension was made to the premises in the 1960s called *The Cromwell Room* and further extensions occurred in 2004. Although Oliver Cromwell had his battery in that area, it is unlikely that his men fired shots from Oliver's Battery to Winchester; more probably the firing range came from the corner of Clifton Hill, off Romsey Road. Cyril Taylor, OBE., licensee for many years, was a city councillor who became Mayor of Winchester in 1973. It is now a *Marston's PLC* venue known simply as *The Stanmore* with the extension called *The Cromwell Suite*.

71. *The Stanmore*, Stanmore Lane. opened in 1933 as the *Stanmore Hotel*.　　　*Photo: Author*

The *New Queen's Head* in Stanmore Lane takes the place of the old *Queen's Head* in Upper Brook Street (see section IV of this chapter). It was built in 1956 for *Strong & Co. of Romsey Ltd.* at the cost of over £25,000. The official opening of the hostelry took place on 4 January 1957. The pub now belongs to the *Enterprise Inns* group.

72. *New Queen's Head*, Stanmore Lane, built in 1956, takes the place of *The Queen's Head*, Upper Brook Street, demolished in the late 1950s.　　　*Photo: Author*

SECTION XI
Staple Gardens, Cross Street, St. George's Street and Jewry Street

I return to the heart of Winchester once more and start with Staple Gardens, or to give its correct title of Staple Garden, which name derives from the word "staple" meaning "a fibre of wool or cotton". The Winchester staple started in 1326 and was one of the ten sites in England where wool could be bought and sold for export. After the 14th century the area was used as a rubbish dump until Sheep Fairs came along which lasted up to the 18th century. It developed as a street in the 19th-century with the building of houses that remain there to this day. Consequently a pub was erected by 1860 known as *New Inn,* changing to *Staple Inn* during the early part of the 1960s. The pub closed in 1973 and the premises remained empty for a number of years. As part of a housing project in 2003 the building was converted into three dwellings (27, 27a and 28). This was a *Courage* pub.

73. *New Inn,* Staple Gardens. Name changed to *Staple Inn* in the early 1960s. The pub closed in 1973. Divided into three private houses in 2003.   *Photo: Author*

Cross Street connects Staple Gardens to Tower Street and on the site of St. Paul's Place, opposite Minters Court, stood the *Blacksmith's Arms* which started as a beer-house in 1880 but within a few years the property became a public house. It was so named because a forge stood close by where horses were shod. Next door to the pub, which closed in 1915, was a bakery!

Before we travel along Jewry Street, I should mention a couple of pubs which existed in St. George's Street during the later part of the 19th century and into the 20th-century, other than *The George Tap* mentioned in chapter 6. The *Plumber's Arms* stood on the site now occupied by the shops and The Winchester Centre known as the Casson Block, named after Sir Hugh Casson who designed this complex in the 1960s. The pub closed in 1888.

Opposite the rear of *The George Hotel*, next to the George Garage, stood *The George Shades*. The pub started in 1887 and ceased trading in 1922. This was one of the licensed premises where I needed help! Apparently, "the Shades" was originally a name for wine and beer vaults with a drinking-bar, either underground or sheltered from the sun by an arcade. This could have applied to this pub, the cellar-bar being "shaded" by the hotel. An alternative theory is that the word "shades" was another meaning for Hades "the underworld abode of the souls of the dead".

Jewry Street is so named as this area, stretching down to Royal Oak Passage, was the home of the Jewish community and traders until they were expelled from the kingdom in 1290 during the reign of Edward I. The reason is given in Section III of this chapter. Their synagogue stood approximately where Toni & Guy's ladies hairdressing salon is today.

Pitkin's Wine Bar (No.3), now Mr. So restaurant, was from 1908 to 1937 E. Batchellor & Son's sweet shop when Mr. Kingsley Dennis took over the business until the late 1950s. The premises then became D.P. Selfe & Co. stationers. Next door (No.4) is *Green's Wine Bar;* this building was from 1920 used by F.B. Heathcote-Ride & Co. chemists and photographic dealers. Mr. Heathcote-Ride, an amateur cine-photographer, took several films of important events in Winchester during the 1930s which are now housed at Wessex Sound & Film Archive, part of Hampshire Record Office. Mr. J. D. Brazier, chemist, acquired the business in the 1950s.

Lane Fox, estate agents, now occupy the building used from 1926 as the City Restaurant transforming into *The City Tavern* in the early 1950s. Previous to 1926 the premises were occupied by Dumpers Ltd., famous for their restaurant on the corner of Market Street and High Street.

DimT Chinese Restaurant, formerly *Savannah Café/Bar,* was Hodders of Winchester, house furnishers, from 1930 to the late 1970s. Previously Matthew & Sons, cabinet makers and upholsterers, occupied the premises.

Almost adjoining the DimT is the independently-owned *Mix Bars*, so-called because "By day Health Juice, Smoothies and Alternative Teas are served" whilst "By night Cocktails and Champagne" attract visitors to this new style drinking venue which opened on 22 June 2006. For many years the premises were owned by Millets, Outfitters, prior to being converted into a photocopying centre in 1980. Copyman took over in 1985 and continued until 2005. They now trade from the rear of premises in Charlecote Mews

Jewry Street was also known as Gaol Street because the old city gaol stood on the site now occupied by *The Old Gaolhouse*, another "modern" pub of Winchester run by the chain of *J.D. Wetherspoon* public houses. There has been a gaol on this site since the 1200s and the pub is housed within part of the old city gaol built in 1788, the debtors wing along the street frontage being added in 1805 to the design of George Moneypenny, a well-known architect. The gaol moved to its present position at the top of Romsey Road in 1849. The premises were occupied for many years by Wm. Dibben & Sons. ironmongers before Habels, house furnishers, took over. When excavations

74. *The Old Gaolhouse*, Jewry Street, is housed within part of the old city gaol built in 1788, the debtors wing along the street frontage being added in 1805. The boozer, part of *J.D. Wetherspoon* chain of public houses, opened in 1997.   *Photo: Author*

were carried out, before the pub opened in 1997, passageways were found leading to Warrens, stationers in High Street, from this site. The reason? Warrens was originally the police station! There is reputed to be a ghost in the cellar of the pub; possibly a prisoner in his cell trying to escape!

Founded by Tim Martin in 1978 Wetherspoon's slogan is "great beer – great conversation". No music is played and no TV screens can be seen. Where does the name J.D. Wetherspoon come from? The founder of the 657-pub chain hails from New Zealand where he attended boarding-school. The house master, J.D. Wetherspoon, very rarely gave Tim a good report; he would not get far in life – that was said to me by a certain headmaster! Now Tim has his revenge by calling his chain of pubs after his house master! Why no music and TV screens? On arrival in this country Tim went into a pub which was playing loud music with TV screens blazing away. So he set up his first "non-music" and "no TV screens" pub in London in 1978. The rest, as the saying goes, is history!

The premises now occupied by John Lewis of Hungerford, kitchen designs, were for a number of years operated by *Aylward & Sons Ltd.* wine and spirit merchants, until late 1950s when *Tyler & Co. Ltd.* who also had a wine shop in High Street (see section II of this chapter), took over until 1968. First known as *Aylward Blake & Chase* the business started in 1880 in the adjoining premises, originally the north-east wing of the gaol, as "importers of wines and spirits" and advertised in their window "coffee roasted on the premises".

The building, tastefully restored in September 2005, previously Framework, ladies hairdressing salon, and now part of a redevelopment plan by Mohamed Bakhaty, was *The Golden Lion*. The pub had been in existence since before 1860 and lost its licence

75. *The Golden Lion*, Jewry Street, lost its licence in 1907. It then became Jewry Tea Rooms followed by the reception area for Elizabethan Restaurant (now Loch Fyne Fish Restaurant) finally ending up as Framework, ladies hairdressing salon. The premises are scheduled to become a restaurant on completion of the present redevelopment of this area in 2007.

Photo: Author

in 1907. The new *Golden Lion* on Alresford Road took its place (see section I of this chapter). On cessation of the licence the premises became Jewry Tea Rooms. Elizabethan Restaurant, now Loch Fyne Fish Restaurant, acquired the building as a reception area for their customers. The refurbished premises will be a bar and waiting room for a new restaurant opening early in 2008. Before the new development commenced in 2006 an archaeological dig took place in October 2005 and experts discovered well-preserved remains of a medieval town-house and a 600-year-old chalk cellar believed to have belonged to a "well-to-do" city trader. Jewry Street, also called by a third name, that of Shoemaker Street, was occupied, not only by the Jewish community, but by craftsmen such as weavers, carpenters and a bookbinder.

The premises in front of Northgate House, once owned by Richard Moss, were built in 1912 as a garage but in 1926 it was converted, for similar use, into Winchester Cycle & Motor Co. which continued until the late 1970s. The property became a wine store called, appropriately, *Bottoms Up,* part of the *Thresher* chain of wine shops. Plans, however, have been approved for the demolition of the building for "replacement of retail/residential" and the store closed in July 2007.

Incidentally, the roadway in front of Northgate House was looked upon in the 1850s as a short cut to North Walls. Many years later, in the 1970s, it was suggested by the Planning Authority of the city council that a roadway through the "cut" to North Walls could be made with the idea of turning the street in front of the Theatre Royal into a precinct, but the proposals never materialised. However, part of Tower Street at the side of the theatre is pedestrianised now that the new discovery centre is complete.

On the corner of Jewry Street and North Walls stood *The Crown and Cushion* but Richard Moss had the pub and stables rebuilt in 1884, designed by Thomas Stopher Junr. at the cost of £192, renaming it *The Crown Hotel*. The premises could never quite decide whether it was in Jewry Street or North Walls and was not one of Winchester's more lively watering-holes. Sited at the "wrong end" of Jewry Street and the "duller" end of North Walls, trading proved difficult. Consequently, the pub was demolished in 1986 when the present office block was built. Naturally, it was a *Winchester Brewery*, later a *Marston's* pub.

76. *The Crown Hotel* stood on the corner of Jewry Street and North Walls. This photo was taken in the 1890s showing the new hotel (taking the place of *The Crown and Cushion*) with the De Lunn Buildings adjoining. *Photo: Winchester Museums, Winchester City Council*

Richard Moss also built the adjoining De Lunn Buildings, again designed by Thomas Stopher Junr. in 1890 at the cost of £3550. Within the row of five shops at No. 4. Mr. H. L. Barlow, a grocer, also became a wine merchant in 1953 and in 1966 the unit was converted fully into a wine shop known as *H.V. (Vintners) Ltd.* which continued under the name of *Southern Wine Stores* until the 1980s. LD Property Management, residential letting specialists, now occupy the premises.

Why the name of De Lunn? The buildings are said to be named after the alleged Mayor of Winchester of 1184, Florence de Lunn. The mythical name was an invention of John Trussell, Mayor in 1624. Florence de Lunn was almost certainly an error for Laurence de Anne who was mayor in 1284. The mayoralty of Winchester is the oldest in the country outside London and the first mayor of the city occurs on 5 April 1200 during the first year of King John's reign and he was probably Elias Westman. There are two roads named after these gentlemen on the Weeke Estate – Trussell Close and Crescent and Westman Road. Mayor-making still takes place every year in May.

SECTION XII
Sussex Street and Upper High Street

The monument standing between the division of Sussex Street and Upper High Street was erected in 1759 by the Society of Natives to mark the spot where money was exchanged for goods at the time of the 1665 plague. A pub was built on that divided area between the two streets in the mid 19th-century called, appropriately, *The Monument*. The name changed to *The Castle Hotel* in 1909 as it faced Hampshire County Council's offices, built on the site of Winchester Castle. The words "Winchester Brewery Co. Ltd." appeared on top of the front wall. It closed in the late 1970s and became a Berni Inn, followed by a Chinese restaurant known as Charles House which is now at No.3 Eastgate Street. The building was demolished in 2001 for the construction of luxury apartments, on condition that the front elevation was to be rebuilt to its original design. This was done, except the builders added an additional level! The complex opened in 2004 and is known as Charles House.

77. *The Monument* public house stood between Sussex Street and Upper High Street; renamed *The Castle Hotel* in 1909. It closed in the late 1970s and became a Berni Inn followed by a Chinese restaurant. Demolished in 2001 and rebuilt in 2003/4 as luxury apartments, with the front elevation almost to the original design. The property is known as Charles House. *Photo: Author*

On the right-hand side of Sussex Street is Ashburton Court and the Tower Street multi-storey car-park. The whole area of shops and houses was demolished in the 1960s including two pubs. The *Sussex Arms* (at one time known as *Sussex Tavern*) stood opposite Newburgh Street and closed in 1960. The *Nag's Head,* a small pub, standing on the corner of Sussex Street with an entrance in Westgate Lane, closed in 1931. There was, apparently, a large finger sign painted on the wall saying "To the Tap".

On the corner of Sussex Street and Gladstone Street was a lovely pub by the name of *Gladstone Arms,* named after William Ewart Gladstone (1809-98), the greatest British reforming statesman of the 19th century; he was Prime Minister on four occasions but not a favourite of Queen Victoria – she preferred his chief opponent, Benjamin Disraeli (1804-81). The pub had unusual coloured tiles on the front fascia and belonged to *Eldridge Pope.* It closed in 1967 and was demolished in 1973 along with houses in that street and the whole of Ashley Terrace for redevelopment of the area including the construction of Gladstone Street car-park.

The *Criterion,* a *Colson* pub, commenced in 1885 and closed in 1914. It was here that the licensee was fined in 1898 for keeping his pub open during "prohibited hours" (see chapter 1). The premises stood approximately where the entrance to Hampshire Record Office is today. The property next door at No. 35 traded as a small temperance hotel for 10 years between 1895 and 1905. I expect, by that year, the proprietor had endured enough from his neighbour and customers!

There were two pubs in Upper High Street, the first being *The Morning Star* which was run by *Courage & Co.* After closure in the late 1950s, the premises became the Zin Yar Chinese Restaurant. It is still one today under the name of Charles House Fusion, a Thai and Japanese restaurant. The pub sign, firmly attached to the front wall, now reads "Charles House Fusion".

Although I was born just round the corner in what was known as Newburgh Place, now part of Newburgh Street, I cannot remember a pub called *Fox & Hounds,* now private houses at Nos. 17 & 18 Upper High Street. No wonder – the pub closed in 1914! When I inspected the properties I could see the archway over the front of the houses which was originally the entrance to the pub.

When I did the pub tour in August 2005, the owner of No. 8 Newburgh Place, where I was born, put a plaque on the front wall!

SECTION XIII
North View, St. Paul's Hill, Western Road and Lower Stockbridge Road

Walk over Oram's Arbour, where there was an Iron Age settlement c.100 BC and you come to North View. On the corner with Middle Road is a private dwelling. This was *The Volunteer Inn,* which had been in existence since before 1880 and closed during the 1970s. Painted on the wall were the words "The Volunteer Inn" and over the entrance the word "Marston's", the successor to *Winchester Brewery.*

Descending Clifton Hill, on the corner with St. Paul's Hill, is the *Railway Inn,* built in 1883 although the railway came to Winchester in June 1839. Famous for its "gig" nights under the title "*Live at The Railway*" the boozer is opposite the car-park which used to be the goods yard and local legend tells that the music-room was originally built as a stable for livestock being transported through to the nearby railway station.

The music-room later evolved into a skittles alley. The venue got a facelift in October 2005 with new video juke-box, TV screen, fruit machines, pool table et al. A lady dressed in a Victorian costume is said to haunt one of the upstairs rooms. The pub now belongs to *Marston's PLC*.

78. The *Railway Inn*, St. Paul's Hill, built in 1883, is famous for its "gig" nights under the title of "*Live at The Railway*".   *Photo: Author*

On the corner of Western Road with Cheriton Road is *The Fulflood Arms*. Built by *Winchester Brewery* in 1871, the front fascia, like *The Gladstone Arms*, has the design of dark green coloured tiles with the words "Winchester Brewery Co. Ltd" and "The Fulflood Arms" embossed thereon. The original *Marston's* pumps are still in use. It is now a *Greene King* pub.

The building on the corner of Elm Road and Lower Stockbridge Road was erected in 1881 as a family hotel for John Wakeford with an accessway leading to the large yard at the rear which contained stables and a barn where horses were tethered. The only form of transport for delivery of goods in those days, other than by rail, was by horse. The goods yard of the railway was, in fact, almost opposite the hotel, which is now used as a car-park. The stables, with a loft door for storage of hay and its cobbled floor is still used today by the present owners, M.J. Brentnall & Son Ltd., building contractors. The premises, known as the *Old Red Deer*, was converted into a public house in 1916 with the *Lion Brewery* operating the venue until 1933 when *Strong & Co. of Romsey Ltd.* took over. The pub closed in 1983 and Michael Brentnall then purchased the property and divided it into two units which are now occupied by NFU Mutual and Cartridge Plus, computer suppliers.

There were two off-licences in Lower Stockbridge Road, virtually opposite each other – one of them still exists today. This is on the corner of Western Road and known locally as *The Omega Wine & Spirit Stores* which commenced in the latter part of the

79. *The Fulflood Arms*, on the corner of Cheriton Road and Western Road, built in 1871. The front fascia has the design of dark green coloured tiles.   *Photo: Author*

19th century. Operated at one time by *Welsh & Co. Ltd.* of *Hyde Abbey Brewery* (see chapter 3), in recent years it was part of *Unwins* chain of wine shops until December 2005 when the company went into liquidation but now the premises are part of the *Thresher* chain, following their take-over in receivership. The property was, however, converted into an Interior Design shop for a few years before reverting back to an off-licence.

On the other side of Lower Stockbridge Road, almost opposite the *Old Red Deer* building, was the other off-licence run by *Whitbreads* which commenced in c.1918 and continued until the 1980s. The premises were then converted into an Interior Design shop by the same firm who moved over the road – they must have had a liking for off-licences! The property is still used for the same line of business by a different firm going under the name of Individual Interior Design.

SECTION XIV
Upper Stockbridge Road, Weeke, Harestock and Springvale

Climbing the hill in Stockbridge Road we come to the *Roebuck Inn* which dates prior to 1835. At one time this pub belonged to *Young & Co.* of *Twyford Brewery* (see chapter 5). Painted on the front wall were the words "Celebrated Twyford Ales & Stout" and over the front doors were the words "Pleasure Gardens", which have now been converted into a car-park! On one of the panels inside the bar are the words "Brickwood's Finest Beers".

Although the pub belonged to *Winchester Brewery* and its successor, *Marston's*, for several years it is quite possible *Brickwoods Brewery* of Portsmouth supplied the "soft" drinks. The *Roebuck Inn* is now part of the *Greene King* chain of pubs.

80. The *Roebuck Inn*, Stockbridge Road, dates prior to 1860. At one time, this pub belonged to *Young & Co.* of *Twyford Brewery.*   *Photo: Author*

Not far from the corner of Stockbridge Road and Stoney Lane stood the *Weeke Hotel,* built in the late 1950s to serve the Weeke Council Estate which commenced in the early 1950s. Later the name changed to *Blightys,* a term used mainly by troops serving abroad; as the song goes "return to dear old Blighty" – England. The interior was decorated in the period of the Second World War which included posters of films featuring popular "pin-ups" such as Hollywood stars Betty Grable and Jane Russell. Another change of name followed, that of *The Chimneys* before the pub was demolished in 2005. The site is at present vacant pending an appeal by German-based Aldi Discount Store, who arrived in Britain in 1990, and are seeking to build one of their stores on the site. The pub originally belonged to *Whitbreads*.

Among the row of shops in Stoney Lane built in the late 1950s is a wine shop, originally run by Keith Bros. until 1987, but is now operated by the *Thresher* chain.

Going over the hill from Bereweeke Avenue we come to the Harestock private housing estate developed in the early 1960s and built on farmland which stretched down to Harestock Road. Most of the roads are named after villages in Hampshire like Amport, Buriton and Priors Dean. In this road stands the *March Hare*, built in the late 1960s and was first operated by *Courage* but now belongs to *Enterprise Inns*. The pub, modern in design compared to other watering-holes in Winchester, blends well with the surrounding dwellings on this estate. It was completely refurbished in August 2006.

On the city boundary lies the Springvale estate, which like other estates in and

81. The *March Hare*, Priors Dean Road, Harestock, built in the 1960s.　　*Photo: Author*

around Winchester, has expanded over the years. On the corner of Springvale Road and Lovedon Lane stands *The King Charles* pub, originally known as *Springvale Hotel*, built in 1919. The pub belonged to *Gales Brewery* but, since the take-over, it is part of the *Fuller's* chain from Chiswick.

82. *The King Charles*, on the corner of Springvale Road and Lovedon Lane, originally called *Springvale Hotel*, was built in 1919.　　*Photo: Author*

SECTION XV
Andover Road and Station Hill

Coming into Winchester on the right-hand side of Andover Road to the corner with Boscobel Road stands the *Jolly Farmer*. The original building dated from the early 1800s but the pub was rebuilt c.1904 on the site of the Aliens Gallows. Close by the Andover Road railway bridge was Gallows Hill where public executions took place from c.1790. Inside the pub are reminders of those days with a replica of a hangman's noose in a glass frame. On one of the walls is a list of some of the prisoners, dragged from the place of sentence, to be executed on the scaffold at Gallows Hill from c.1790 to 1862. These executions were witnessed by crowds who took great pleasure in a good hanging, laughing at the convicted criminals.

There is also recorded the story of a ghost that walks the *Jolly Farmer*. Apparently Harry Whitley was executed on Gallows Hill for petty theft, that of four capons and three hens. Whitley was sentenced to be hanged; he pleaded "benefit of clergy" which was the right for all condemned persons who could read or write and were looked upon as scholars, having their hands branded instead of the ultimate penalty. Whitley did not possess this benefit and, as a mere poultry thief, was automatically condemned to death on the scaffold at Gallows Hill. He tried to escape his doom by pleading "benefit of clergy". Whitley, when tested, failed to qualify and the sessions condemned him to death and he was hanged on Gallows Hill. His ghost is said to haunt the watering-hole. Originally a *Strong & Co. of Romsey Ltd.* pub it now belongs to *Greene King*.

83. The *Jolly Farmer*, Andover Road, rebuilt c.1904 on the site of the Aliens Gallows. Inside the pub are reminders of public executions at nearby Gallows Hill which took place from c.1790 to 1862.
Photo: Author

On the other side of the Andover Road bridge parallel to the railway is Andover Road Retail Park, erected in the early 1990s on the site of buildings once occupied by H.J. Coombs & Co. Ltd., wholesale fruit merchants, and Webbs Frozen Foods Ltd. Among the four units is *Majestic Wine Warehouse* belonging to the company of the same name who operate 133 wine stores in this country and three "Wine & Bar World" superstores in France.

On the corner of Andover Road and Lower Stockbridge Road stands *The Albion* which dates from the mid-19th century. It is now a *Punch Tavern* pub.

84. *The Albion*, on the corner of Andover Road and Lower Stockbridge Road, dates from the mid-19th century.   *Photo: Author*

Going up Station Hill we come to a gravelled area forming part of Hampshire Record Office. On this site stood *The Railway Tavern* which commenced before 1873. On the front wall were the words "Eldridge Pope & Co's Huntsman Ales & Stout". The pub was demolished in the late 1970s to make way for the new Hampshire Record Office. As mentioned in section I of this chapter *The Railway Tavern* was only the second pub in his long career as a publican that Bert Spicer was licensee, the first being *The Great Western Hotel* in Bridge Street.

Just above this *Eldridge Pope* pub stands the The Register Office for Births, Deaths and Marriages. This building, dating from before 1873, was originally known as *Railway Refreshment Inn,* the name changing to the *South Western Inn* in 1920. The pub closed in 1992 for conversion into its present-day use controlled by Hampshire County Council.

The first railway company to run a line through Winchester was the London and South Western starting with the section from Winchester to Southampton which opened in June 1839 but the complete route from London to Southampton opened eleven months later in May 1840. It is ironic that the South Western Railway operated the first trains, later to become known as Southern Railway, then British Rail and now we have reverted to South West Trains, operated by a bus company -Stagecoach!

85. The *South Western Inn*, Station Hill, originally known as *Railway Refreshment Inn*. Now The Register Office for Births, Deaths and Marriages.   *Photo: Author*

SECTION XVI
Saxon Road and Hyde Street

There has to be a pub in Winchester named after that great Saxon King who ruled his kingdom of Wessex from the city, *The King Alfred,* appropriately situated in Saxon Road. A brick and flint cottage in Hyde Church Path was demolished and with land adjoining, *Winchester Brewery* purchased the site in 1897 for £550 so that a pub could be erected. This was completed on 3 January 1898 at the cost of £1220.

There was opposition from residents and the Rector of St. Bartholomew Church with regard to the building of a pub in that part of the parish! Mr. Shenton of Shentons, solicitors, whose offices are now Star Lane House, Staple Gardens, (the original name of the street being Star Lane), appeared for the brewery at the hearing for the grant of a licence whilst Mr. White, of White & Nash, now White *&* Bowker, solicitors of St. Peter Street, appeared for the objectors – Mr. Shenton won! The first licensee in 1898 was James Whitlock. It is now a *Greene King* pub and is famous for winning floral display awards and winning pub quizzes!

The North Gate which stood at the top of Hyde Street was demolished in 1756. Just below, and opposite Swan Lane, stands *The White Swan* public house, formerly part of *Winchester Brewery* (see chapter 3) which has been in existence since 1784, and at some time in the past affectionately referred to as *The Mucky Duck.*

Much of the information for the Domesday Book (AD1086) was collated at Winchester and it is possible that part of the Book was written in the tenement, now the site of *The White Swan.* In the cellar of the pub is a stone wall from the medieval building. There is a list of landlords from 1784 in the billiard room, the first being

86. *The King Alfred*, Saxon Road, built in 1898, is named after the great Saxon King who ruled
his kingdom of Wessex from the city.   *Photo: Author*

Thomas Tuckle; also on display in the room is a framed copy of the Winchester pubs
story (see chapter 7). A great deal of the decorated woodwork dating from the early
13th century can be seen around the watering-hole which, naturally, is now a *Greene
King* pub.

Incidentally, Swan Lane was the original medieval route leading towards the North
Gate and busy with carts, horses and pedestrian traffic before City Road became a
thoroughfare in the 19th century. At one time it was known as Swine Lane denoting a
rather filthy thoroughfare!

87. *The White Swan*, Hyde Street, has been in existence since 1784, and in the past affectionately
referred to as *The Mucky Duck*.   *Photo: Author*

The property adjoining *Hyde Abbey Brewery*, Wyeth House now stands on the site (see chapter 3), was formed into a hotel/pub in 1901 for *Welsh & Co. Ltd.* the owners of the brewery to the design of Thomas Stopher Junr. at the cost of £1930. An old brewery originally stood on this site. *Hyde Abbey Hotel* opened in 1903 and closed in 1964. The 1934 auction particulars described the property as having "7 bedrooms, Guests' Sitting Room, Coffee Room, Salon Bar, Tap Room" et al. The premises are now occupied by Sarsen Press. The second pub by the name of *Brewers' Arms* stood close by but this closed in 1897.

88. *Hyde Abbey Hotel*, Hyde Street. Trading from 1903 to 1964. Now the home of Sarsen Press, the printers of this book. *Photo: Author*

The *Prince of Wales* stood on the corner of Hyde Street and Hyde Close and had been in existence since before 1880, possibly taking the place of the former pub by that name which stood in The Square and is referred to in the 1859 directory. The present *Prince of Wales*, an *Eldridge Pope* pub, closed in 2003 and the premises is being converted into dwelling accommodation.

The two pubs which 'foxed' everyone, as mentioned in the Acknowledgements, were *The George Shades* and *The 3d Whip*. The former was easily solved (see section XI of this chapter) but where was *The 3d. Whip* mentioned in the story contained in chapter 7? Verna Gregory came up with the answer. Apparently, the anonymous author did not quite get his facts right. *The 3d. Whip* was a "nickname" given to a tavern called *The Blue Posts*, situated at 56 Hyde Street, and was derived from a drink made on the premises consisting of a pint of beer, costing 2d., and a pennyworth of gin – hence the 3d. whip. The landlord concocting this "special" was Harry Gauntlett who ran the small pub from at least 1859 to 1892. The property is now a private house by the name of "Tavern Cottage" and is positioned between *The Hyde Tavern* and Hyde Parish Hall.

89. The *Prince of Wales* on the corner of Hyde Street and Hyde Close had been in existence since before 1880. Closed in 2003. The premises is being converted into dwelling accommodation.   *Photo: Author*

Finally, in this long saga of pubs, I conclude with what is reputed to be the city's oldest pub – *The Hyde Tavern*. Built in medieval times it was a house until the 1700s, when the property became a tavern. It now belongs to *Admiral Taverns* chain of pubs.

The Hyde Tavern has its origins in the days of King Alfred. Henry I built the monastery of Hyde Abbey nearby and no doubt many weary pilgrims and travellers found a watering-hole of some sort on the site as a convenient source of refreshment and lodging.

90. The one that nearly got away! *The Blue Posts (The 3d. Whip)*, Hyde Street, positioned between *The Hyde Tavern* and Hyde Parish Hall. A small pub from at least 1859 to 1892. Now a private house known as "Tavern Cottage".   *Photo: Author*

I complete this chapter and book with a final ghost story. It is said that many, many years ago the landlord of *The Hyde Tavern* turned away a poor woman on a cold winter's night. Whether the inn was full or she had insufficient money, we do not know, but according to the story, the woman's body was found the next morning. She had died from cold and hunger. Her ghost may still haunt the inn where residents and guests have found their sleep disturbed by a phantom intruder who pulls away their blankets. How sad!

On a slightly brighter note a project entitled "Hyde 900", scheduled for May-December 2010, will mark the 900th anniversary of the foundation of Hyde Abbey, the burial place of King Alfred the Great (as well as his wife Queen Alswitha and son King Edward). It aims to be a community-led festival which will celebrate the history of Hyde, explore the locality and environment and showcase the wide variety of talents of the people who live in the area. Above all, it aims to be plenty of fun. No doubt the pumps of *The King Alfred* and *The Hyde Tavern* will be working overtime during those eight months!

91. *The Hyde Tavern*, Hyde Street. Built in medieval times, it was a house until the 1700s when the property became a pub.   *Photo: Author*

APPENDIX
The Greene King Story

Although the *Greene King* brewery is not based in Hampshire the Company does own many of the city's public houses which originally belonged to *Winchester Brewery* and their successors *Marston's,* so it is only fair to mention the Suffolk brewery in this book and relate some details of the brewery's history.

Benjamin Greene (1780-1860) came to the ancient market town of Bury St. Edmunds in 1799 at the early age of 19 and six years later, in 1805, he teamed up with William Buck, a 60-year old yarn maker, to purchase *Wrights Brewery* on the corner of Crown Street and Westgate Street. They renamed it *Westgate Brewery* and that name still applies today.

The business greatly expanded during the time that Benjamin's son Edward took control from 1836 to 1858. In that year Edward passed the day-to-day running of the brewery to his son Walter along with his nephew W. Lake and manager William Pead.

In 1868 Frederick William King, a farmer and maltster, founded *St. Edmunds Brewery* next door to the Greene's *Westgate Brewery.* An agreeement was reached 19 years later in 1887 when Frederick King joined forces with the Greene family; subsequently the name of Greene King & Sons Ltd. was born.

On the opposite side of Westgate Street stands Bury's Georgian Theatre Royal which opened in 1819 and is the third oldest working theatre in the country. Its fortunes, however, began to decline in the early 1900s; *Greene King* purchased the venue in 1920, paid off the debts and the company's Chairman, Edward Lake, tried for five years to keep it going as a live theatre. This failed and the venue closed on 20 April 1925. As owners of the theatre *Greene King* were in a strong position to use the stage and auditorium as a cask warehouse, and this they did from 1928 to 1961 when a restoration appeal was launched and the brewers offered the theatre to the trustees at a peppercorn rent for 21 years. Meanwhile, the barrels were rolled out and the builders moved in! After fund raising and refurbishment was completed the theatre reopened on 1 April 1965. Forward ten years to 23 May 1975 *Greene King* granted a 999-year lease to the National Trust for the traditional annual rent of a peppercorn who thereby acquired its first working theatre. One of the instigators for negotiations on behalf of the brewers was Sir Hugh Greene, Chairman of the company and former Director of the BBC (1960-69).

In the 1950s and 1960s *Greene King* staved off take-over bids from larger companies, the Directors being determined to remain independent in a time of big brewery take-overs.

In recent years further expansions have taken place including an investment of over £2 million in 2004 resulting in new fermenting vessels being installed, the refurbishment of mash tuns and the brewhouse which was built in 1938.

Since 1954 *Greene King Brewing Company* have acquired several breweries and consequently the brewers have emerged as one of the largest companies within the UK brewing industry operating more than 2,400 pubs.

The most popular brands of beer are Greene King IPA, Abbot Ale, Old Speckled Hen and Ruddles County. The Visitor Centre is situated next to the brewery, where, in 1987 a 60-barrel copper, which was used by the *Westgate Brewery* in the 1920s, was placed on the street outside the Visitor Centre.

(I am grateful to the Visitor Centre of Greene King Brewery Company for the information contained in the Appendix)

Postscript: The smallest pub in the country is at Bury St. Edmunds – just 7 feet all round, it is called *The Nutshell!*

EPILOGUE

Although, as I mentioned in chapter 2, the number of watering-holes may have diminished over the years, those that are still functioning at a "community" level, are very much part of the social way of life, where friends and neighbours meet over a drink, coupled sometimes with a game of pool or darts. The pub is also a source for information, contacts....and local gossip!

Innkeepers today are not only "mine hosts" with their customary bar staff but, in most cases, their responsibility involves many other tasks; i.e. catering arrangements for wedding receptions, employing chefs to deal with the restaurant side of the business and, of course, if the pub is large enough to accommodate tourists who prefer staying in the atmosphere of an English pub, then this adds to the load of work of the licensees.

Incidentally, according to the *Oxford English Dictionary*, the term "mine host" originates from a 13th-century rule that "you put myn before a vowel or an H" and this continued into the 18th century. There is also a reference to this phrase in Shakespeare's *The Merry Wives of Windsor*.

So, when you next visit your local pub, remember the hard work and long hours put in by the landlord/landlady and their partners.

By the way, if your "local" happens to be steeped in history, consider its background and raise a glass to the ghosts of tipplers past!

ABOUT THE TRUST

In the late 1950s Winchester City Council implemented their scheme to "modernise" the city, which affected many properties in the streets of the city centre. Although some dwellings were beyond restoration, the majority could have, and should have, been saved.

Horrified by the council's decision to proceed with their plans, five prominent citizens met and discussed what course of action to take. This resulted in the formation of a group with the sole aim to try and prevent the council from desecrating the city centre. Consequently, in 1957 The Winchester Preservation Trust came into being, registered with the Charity Commission No. 251798.

Their first task in that year was to spearhead the regeneration of Canon Street, which the city council had earmarked for demolition. Thankfully, the street was saved and today it is described in estate agents' particulars as "a desirable residential area of Winchester".

The following year all eyes fell on The Brooks, starting with Upper Brook Street. The Trust prepared specifications for the repair of *The Queen's Head* (referred to in section IV of chapter 8) and the adjoining properties. They applied for grant-aid and organized an appeal and petition signed by more than 800 citizens. Although the Trust raised sufficient money to save the buildings and despite the view of The Ministry of Works that the properties should be saved and preserved in the national interest, the city council demolished them together with other dwellings in the street. A similar pattern followed with properties in Middle and Lower Brook Streets.

Over the years, however, the Trust has been successful in rescuing premises, which otherwise would have been destroyed, including opposing an application to the Department of the Environment by the city council to demolish Nos. 52/54 Upper Brook Street which date from 1820. These buildings, now numbered 30/32, are now used partly as the registered offices of the Trust and partly for residential purposes but their first use was as the Heritage Centre which opened in July 1983. The following year a grant of £12,000 was awarded by the Carnegie UK Trust for the creation of a permanent interpretive exhibition at the Heritage Centre. A video presentation entitled *Winchester Heritage* was an added attraction. The Centre closed in September 1997 and work was carried out in 1999 to convert the buildings into offices and a residential dwelling.

In 2000 the name of the Trust changed to The City of Winchester Trust "to reflect more closely the objective of continuing care for the City whilst accepting appropriate changes".

During the last 50 years, the Trust has not only kept a "watchful eye" on buildings which may be victims of demolition proposals; they have also participated in several important issues concerning Winchester such as the M3 extension Enquiry, the Bar End Park & Ride extension Enquiry and more recently the Silver Hill Development Brief and the listing of the Hockley Viaduct.

A series of booklets about Winchester's streets was published between 1976 and 1988. The first Chippindale Venture to mark the contribution to education made by the late Frank Chippindale, RIBA, was launched in 1989 and, this project involving children from local schools, continued to 1998.

The summer evening walks, referred to in the Introduction, for members and friends around different parts of the city have proved very popular over the years. The Awards Scheme to attract architectural designs of new or converted buildings was launched in 1983.

Different groups within the Trust membership, specialising in various aspects of the city, meet regularly especially the Planning Appraisal Group, who peruse and inspect all applications within the six City wards submitted to the City's Planning Department and advise the Trust Council on their findings.

So, as The City of Winchester Trust celebrates its 50th anniversary, citizens may rest assured that the Trust has their interests very much at heart!

92. The Heritage Centre, Upper Brook Street. Registered Office of The City of Winchester Trust Ltd. Originally two houses dating from 1820. *Photo: Author*

93. Michael Sinker, the city's longest-serving publican, 35 years at *The Bakers Arms*, raises his glass to toast the 50th anniversary of the formation of The City of Winchester Trust.

Photo: Author

94. The launch of this book (1st edition) at the *Mash Tun* by BBC broadcaster Peter White, MBE. In the photo L to R: Sue Nelmes (Mayor of Winchester), Patricia Edwards (Chairman of The City of Winchester Trust), Phil Yates and Peter White. *Photo: Hampshire Chronicle*

BIBLIOGRAPHY

Badcock, Colin: *Winchester* (The Pevensey Press) 1988

Baker, John L.: *A Picture of Hampshire* (Robert Hale)1986

Barton, John: *Winchester Yesterday & Today* (Halsgrove) 1998

Carpenter Turner, Barbara: *A History of Winchester* (Phillimore & Co.Ltd.) 1992

Green, Richard D.: *A History of St. Peter's Church Chesil Street* (Winchester Dramatic Society) 2004

Richmond, Lesley/Turton, Alison: *The Brewing Industry – A Guide to Historical Records* (Manchester University Press) 1990

Sermon, David: *The Chapter & The City – 200 years of Freemasonry in Winchester* (David Sermon) 2003

Other Sources of Information

*A History of Winchester Streets (1895-1926) Thomas Stopher Junr.

Directory of Hampshire & the Isle of Wight (William White)1859

Hampshire Chronicle – 4 March 1905 (Richard Moss)

Hampshire Chronicle – 8 May 1926 (Thomas Stopher Junr.)

Hampshire Chronicle – 26 May 1934 (new coach station)

Hampshire Chronicle – 8 November 1985 (*The Blue Boar*)

Hampshire Chronicle – 14 October 2005 (Elizabeth Hickish)

Kelly's Directories of Winchester (1927-1972)

Ordnance Survey Maps – 1869-1873, 1897 and 1909

Proceedings of the Hampshire Field Club & Archaeological Society – Volume XXVII for 1970

The Oxford English Dictionary 2nd Edition Vol XV – Prepared by J.A. Simpson and E.S.C. Weiner (Clarendon Press Oxford) 1989

The Wainscot Book – the Houses of Winchester Cathedral Close and their Interior Decoration AD1660 - AD1800 edited by John Crook – Hampshire Record Office for Hampshire County Council (1984)

Venta Belgarum, The Roman Town of Winchester – Winchester Museums Service (1997)

Warren's Winchester Directories (1880-1974)

Winchester College: Its history, buildings and customs – The Winchester College Archaeological Society (1926)

*Unpublished material held by Hampshire Collection (formerly Local Studies Library)

ACKNOWLEDGEMENTS

Writing books is not an easy task but the end result makes it all worthwhile. To achieve this goal for *Time Gentlemen, Please!* I am indebted to so many people.

Firstly, I would like to thank Patricia Edwards, Chairman of The City of Winchester Trust and fellow Council Members for their encouragement and financial assistance coupled with a generous donation from Jeffrey Smith, a vice-president and a founder member of the Trust. His enthusiasm and knowledge of its early days was extremely valuable.

I am also indebted to past Chairman Roger Backhouse, Q.C. and Chris Pile for their splendid donations towards the cost of the book's publication.

To undertake such a project, researching is of the utmost importance. I am particularly grateful to the staff of Hampshire Collection (formerly the Local Studies Library) for their tremendous help and endless patience. So much so, that I wish to record their names: Alys Blakeway, Robin Freeman, Keith Hayward, Sandy Mounsey, Richard Preston and Val Russell. The staff of Hampshire Record Office were always "on hand" to produce documents, plans and reference books for which I thank them.

Old photographs of buildings which no longer exist have played an essential part in this book and Karen Parker, Curator of Photographs at the former Hyde Historic Resources Centre (part of Winchester Museums Service) produced a varied selection to make sure that the best quality was reproduced. I am indebted to her for this excellent service.

Not being familiar with the modern technology of computers and the internet, I was reliant on Maurice Charrett, Madelaine Smith and Keith Wilson to search the websites for information and I thank them for their excellent service.

Judith Blake was responsible for planning the book and slotting all ninety-four photographs into their right positions. My sincere thanks to her.

It is always advisable to have "on board" reliable proof-readers to scrutinize your manuscript and I am indebted to John Barton, Tony Hill and my wife Joan for helping to carry out this vitally important task.

Sometimes it is necessary to approach occupiers of premises for details relating to the previous use of their property. I could not have found a more charming couple than Pat and Hal Norris whose house at St. Cross was the *Gardener's Arms* (see section VII of chapter 8). I did appreciate their help. The Porter of The Hospital of St. Cross also enlightened me about the brewhouse in the quadrangle (see chapter 3). Thank you for giving me your time. It is always a pleasure visiting that tranquil part of the city.

I spent a pleasant afternoon with Michael Brentnall at the *Old Red Deer* site where he produced plans and an unpublished booklet called *The History of The Old Red Deer* by Annabel Redhead which contained some interesting facts. He also showed me round the yard and the stable building containing the original cobbled floor. I am grateful to him for giving me so much of his time.

Two public or beer-houses perplexed everyone at Hampshire Collection and

Hampshire Record Office – *The George Shades* and *The 3d. Whip*. The solution? Write letters to the *Hampshire Chronicle* and *NewsExtra*; someone is sure to get in touch – and they did! Consequently, the definite meaning of *George Shades* came from our County Librarian, Richard Ward, plus father and son Tom and Myk Cromie (see section XI of chapter 8). I am indebted to them for solving this problem. I almost gave up hope of finding any information about *The 3d. Whip*, but Verna Gregory came up trumps! She not only produced an old book entitled *Hampshire & the Isle of Wight* dated 1859, which gave the correct name of the beer-house, but she also provided the concoction that made up the 3d. Whip! (See section XVI of chapter 8). My sincere thanks to her for coming to my rescue! Her brother David Young supplied details of *The Nag's Head*. I am grateful to him and also to Anthony Bathurst for additional information.

Dealing with past breweries outside Winchester caused a problem until I made contact with Phoebe Merrick of Lower Test Valley Archaeological Study Group (*Strong & Co. of Romsey Ltd*) and Tony Cross of Curtis Museum Alton (*Courage & Co.*) who were able to supply details regarding these breweries. (See chapter 5). I am most grateful to both of them.

My thanks go to all publicans, brewers and hoteliers who gave up so much of their busy working life to assist with this publication.

Finally, and above all, I thank my wife, who in the early days of this project, trudged through the streets of Winchester with me tracking down locations of hostelries that are no longer with us.

Some of the public houses referred to in this book have now been transformed into private dwelling-houses and I should stress that the privacy of their owners must be respected at all times; the mention of a pub which is now a house does not mean that it is open to the public!

PHOTOGRAPHS

Photographs are an important part of any book and assist the reader to understand more clearly the text relating to certain buildings; this is particularly the case concerning the pubs, breweries and hotels of *Time Gentlemen, Please!* I am, therefore, extremely grateful to the following for their permission to reproduce the photographs contained in the book:

Brown, George Roger: p. 56
Hampshire Chronicle: pp. 21, 27, 31, 92, 121
Hampshire County Library: pp. 43, 72, 77, 81, 94
Lower Test Valley Archaeological Study Group: p. 33
Pile, Chris: Front and Back covers
Roberts, Edward: p. 45
Sollars, E.A. (Winchester Museums, Winchester City Council): pp. 40,41
Southwick Brewhouse: p. 37
Winchester Museums, Winchester City Council: pp. 13, 17, 18, 19, 24, 26, 31, 45, 83, 102

KEY

The numbers on the map coincide with the list of illustrations on pages 6-8.

● Pub and 'taps' (past and present)
⊗ Breweries (all past)
✱ Hotels (past and present)
✳ Wine stores and off-licences (past and present)
X Malt-houses (all past)
+ Brewhouses (all past)

GORDON RD

PARK AVE

NORTH WALLS

58

PARCHMENT ST

UPPER BROOK ST

MIDDLE BROOK ST

LOWER BROOK ST

DURNGATE

37
38
WALES STREET

42

56
55
57

5

FRIARSGATE

41

CHESTER RD

32

34 35
ALRESFORD ROAD

48
54

HIGH STREET

46

WATER LANE

ST JOHNS ST

MAGDALEN HILL

59
47
45
44
X

MARKET LANE

BROADWAY

43

24

EASTGATE ST

40
36

QUARE

CATHEDRAL

39
33

COLEBROOK ST

CHESIL ST

4

DEANERY +

+ PILGRIMS' HALL

COLLEGE ST

⊗ WINCHESTER
COLLEGE

31
30
29

WHARF HILL

BRIDGE STREET

28

THE STORY OF THE MAP

One morning in May 2005 Chris Pile knocked on the front door of my house and said: "I thought you would like this map I have prepared for your summer evening walks on the pubs, breweries and hotels of Winchester as a guidance especially as so many of the venues have since vanished". I thanked him and found the map useful for the walks. So, it has come full circle and now serves as a record for the book, although revised for the purposes of printing.

The map, not to scale, is purely for identification purposes only. The approximate position of every venue mentioned in the book is marked by the symbol indicated on the key at the top right-hand corner of the map.

It was not possible to mark the venues in Bereweeke Road, Weeke and Harestock but the symbols apply to the following:

*   *Chantry Mead Hotel,* Bereweeke Road
*   *The Travellers Rest* – Weeke
*   *Harestock Lodge Hotel,* Harestock Road
●   *The Chimneys* – Weeke
❉   Wine Shop, Stoney Lane

Now try and fathom out the positions of the various buildings!

GONE-AND FORGOTTEN

As a postscript to the book, it is interesting to note according to *Pigot & Co's* directory for Winchester of 1824, kindly produced by Jennifer Rosser, that several public houses are mentioned which disappeared from our city streets many years ago. Here are a few names to stimulate the brain!

Angel, Middle Brook Street
Antelope, St. George's Street
Barleymow, The Square
Black Bear, St. George's Street
Five Bells, St. John's Street
Pelican, Colebrook Street
Rodney's Head, St. John's Street
Three Horse Shoes, The Square
Wool Pack, Lower Brook Street

The maltsters of Winchester in 1824 consisted of the following:

Charles Barham, Chesil Street
Richard Barnes, Hyde Street
John Goodchild, Colebrook Street
Richard Harris, Water Lane
and the only lady
Hester Long, Chesil Street

The directory also states that "the city of Winchester has been much improved by appearance since the year 1770, when an Act for paving and lighting the streets was obtained" and "Winchester has very little trade". One hundred and eighty three years later a different story emerges!

ABOUT THE AUTHOR

Phil Yates was born June 1927 in Winchester and received his education at Nethercliffe Preparatory and Peter Symonds schools. In 1943 he was employed by Godwins, solicitors, as "office boy" and remained with the same firm until 1983, rising to the position of Senior Legal Executive. In that year Phil decided to take early retirement from the legal profession and changed careers, becoming Assistant Marketing Manager to the Theatre Royal. Interested in theatre and cinema from an early age, Phil has appeared in many plays and pantomimes with local companies. He was appointed Hon. Archivist and Historian to the Theatre Royal in 1980 and still helps out in the marketing department, as well as being a member of the front of house staff for various shows. In October 2005 Phil was presented with a long-service award by the Mayor of Winchester for 30 years voluntary work at the theatre.

Phil was conscripted to the coal mines in April 1945, and worked at collieries in the Yorkshire coalfields before demobilization in March 1948. He joined The Bevin Boys Association in 1992 and his booklet *The Bevin Boys' Story* was published in 1993 and reprinted in 2004. He co-wrote, with the Vice-President of the Association, Warwick Taylor MBE, a history of the Association called *Digging up the Past* which was published in April 2006.

Phil joined the City of Winchester Trust in 1983 and since 2001 he has been one of the tour guides who conduct Summer Walks for the Trust (see the Introduction).

Since 1989 Phil has written six booklets, five of them about the city and he is now in the process of compiling a book on the history of the Theatre Royal with Madelaine Smith, its Marketing & Development Manager, which will be published in 2008.

He now resides with his wife Joan in Tower Street – not far from the theatre!